CAMBRIDGE LIBRARY COLLECTION

Books of enduring scholarly value

Music

The systematic academic study of music gave rise to works of description, analysis and criticism, by composers and performers, philosophers and anthropologists, historians and teachers, and by a new kind of scholar - the musicologist. This series makes available a range of significant works encompassing all aspects of the developing discipline.

Half a Century of Music in England, 1837-1887

This collection of essays by the music critic Francis Hueffer (1843-1889) is a lively contemporary account of musical life in Victorian England. First published in 1889, it records the influence of leading foreign composers on English music. Ranging from the music of Handel, Gluck and Haydn to Weber, Rossini, and Mendelssohn, composers who have had a lasting influence on the British musical world, Hueffer, who did not live to see the publication of his book, offers a panoramic view of the rapid development of musical culture in England during the nineteenth century. Starting with a historical introduction to the roles played by the Royal Academy and the Royal College of Music, and moving on to the specific contributions of 'new' composers including Berlioz, Wagner and Liszt, this book is a valuable guide to the history and criticism of music in Victorian England as it was understood at the time.

AF076233

Cambridge University Press has long been a pioneer in the reissuing of out-of-print titles from its own backlist, producing digital reprints of books that are still sought after by scholars and students but could not be reprinted economically using traditional technology. The Cambridge Library Collection extends this activity to a wider range of books which are still of importance to researchers and professionals, either for the source material they contain, or as landmarks in the history of their academic discipline.

Drawing from the world-renowned collections in the Cambridge University Library, and guided by the advice of experts in each subject area, Cambridge University Press is using state-of-the-art scanning machines in its own Printing House to capture the content of each book selected for inclusion. The files are processed to give a consistently clear, crisp image, and the books finished to the high quality standard for which the Press is recognised around the world. The latest print-on-demand technology ensures that the books will remain available indefinitely, and that orders for single or multiple copies can quickly be supplied.

The Cambridge Library Collection will bring back to life books of enduring scholarly value (including out-of-copyright works originally issued by other publishers) across a wide range of disciplines in the humanities and social sciences and in science and technology.

Half a Century of Music in England, 1837-1887

Essays Towards a History

FRANCIS HUEFFER

CAMBRIDGE UNIVERSITY PRESS

Cambridge, New York, Melbourne, Madrid, Cape Town, Singapore,
São Paolo, Delhi, Dubai, Tokyo

Published in the United States of America by Cambridge University Press, New York

www.cambridge.org
Information on this title: www.cambridge.org/9781108004725

© in this compilation Cambridge University Press 2009

This edition first published 1889
This digitally printed version 2009

ISBN 978-1-108-00472-5 Paperback

This book reproduces the text of the original edition. The content and language reflect
the beliefs, practices and terminology of their time, and have not been updated.

Cambridge University Press wishes to make clear that the book, unless originally published
by Cambridge, is not being republished by, in association or collaboration with, or
with the endorsement or approval of, the original publisher or its successors in title.

HALF A CENTURY OF MUSIC IN ENGLAND.

HALF A CENTURY

OF

MUSIC IN ENGLAND

1837—1887.

ESSAYS TOWARDS A HISTORY.

BY

FRANCIS HUEFFER.

LONDON: CHAPMAN AND HALL,
LIMITED.
1889.
[*All rights reserved.*]

TO HER MAJESTY

𝔗𝔥𝔢 𝔔𝔲𝔢𝔢𝔫,

THE FRIEND OF MENDELSSOHN,
AND
THE FIRST ENGLISHWOMAN TO RECOGNISE THE GENIUS OF WAGNER,

THIS BOOK

IS BY PERMISSION RESPECTFULLY DEDICATED BY

THE AUTHOR.

PREFACE.

A FEW introductory words as to the title and the contents of the present volume may not seem out of place. The title denotes the plan of a comprehensive work dealing with the history of Music in this country during the reign of Queen Victoria—a reign which, amongst other important events, has witnessed the revival of Music as a national art in England; the contents are a first instalment of such a work, on the reception of which the completion of the whole must largely depend. A chronological arrangement of the vast material at hand, an account of musical events from day to day, from season to season, might have produced a very learned, but would to a certainty have produced a very dull work, useful perhaps to the historian and critic, but religiously shunned by the general public. I have therefore preferred to group dates and facts round certain men of light and leading, and I shall be glad to think that the care and trouble with which those dates and facts have been collected and verified from contemporary sources may not be noticed by the ordinary reader at all.

As a matter of courtesy, I have given the *pas* to the great foreign masters who have visited our shores during the period under notice. How they have fared amongst us, what they have done and left undone, how they have permanently influenced the current of English Music—all this, for the first time, will be discussed in the following pages, with such care and minuteness of research as have not to my knowledge been previously bestowed upon so interesting a subject. Apart from courtesy, it must be owned that the greater portion of musical work in England during the last half-century has been done by foreigners. The premature death of Purcell and the advent of Handel were equally conducive to crushing the singularly rich development of early English Music, and to ushering in a long line of illustrious foreigners, from Handel, and Gluck, and Haydn, to Weber, and Rossini, and Mendelssohn. To these the English nation pinned their faith, withdrawing that faith from native composers, who in consequence no longer believed in themselves; not at least outside the walls, or, more properly speaking, the organ-lofts of churches and cathedrals. Within the last ten years a change for the better has come over English Music, reviving the confidence at once of the worker and of those for whom the work is intended.

With English Music during the last fifty years, and more especially with our contemporary school of composers, I propose to deal in a subsequent volume, provided such a volume should be called for. For purposes of reference I have here thought it sufficient to introduce the separate chapters by a general synopsis of the period, which had previously appeared in *The Fortnightly Review*. Portions of the chapter on Liszt are republished from the same periodical, while some of the materials of the Wagner chapter were previously used for an article in *The Quarterly Review* of July, 1888.

NOTE.

The ink was scarcely dry upon the final pages of this book, when the hand which wrote them ceased work for ever; a wide circle of friends mourned the sudden removal from their midst of an amiable, clear-minded, and highly-gifted companion; and musical art in England sustained a loss the full extent of which will be realised as time goes on. It has been the earnest endeavour of the friend who has undertaken the task of preparing the present volume for the press, to avoid all unnecessary alteration, and to follow in the minutest detail what he believes would have been the writer's wishes. Readers will observe with satisfaction that the author had chosen for this first instalment of his work a section of the subject upon which, by reason of his superior knowledge and known predilections, he was entitled to speak with special authority; and it may be regarded as a singular coincidence that the last chapter should have been devoted to a declaration of certain opinions, his able advocacy of which during many years past has contributed not a little towards the making of that history it was his intention to write.

H. A. RUDALL.

London, *March*, 1889.

CONTENTS.

CHAPTER I.
INTRODUCTORY—GENERAL MUSIC DURING THE QUEEN'S REIGN IN ENGLAND 1

CHAPTER II.
WAGNER IN ENGLAND 29

CHAPTER III.
LISZT IN ENGLAND 85

CHAPTER IV.
BERLIOZ IN ENGLAND 151

CHAPTER V.
CONCLUSION 235

HALF A CENTURY OF MUSIC IN ENGLAND.

1837-1887.

CHAPTER I.

INTRODUCTORY—GENERAL MUSIC DURING THE QUEEN'S REIGN IN ENGLAND.

It is no exaggeration to say that with the exception perhaps of natural science, both in the applied and the philosophic sense, there is no branch of human knowledge, or of human art, in which the change that the half-century of the Queen's reign has wrought, is so marked as it is in the spirit of music. I advisedly say the spirit of music, for with the practice and the productiveness of the art I shall have to deal later on. By the spirit of music is here understood the spirit in which music is regarded both by the artists who practise it, and by the amateurs who enjoy it in a more or less active manner. Fifty years ago, music in the higher sense was, to the majority of the people, an all but unknown quantity. The existing concert societies in London were few in number, and appealed almost exclusively to their own members, drawn from what then would have been called " the nobility and gentry," and what in modern parlance we may describe as " the classes;" the masses being left out in the cold. Still more was this true of the Italian Opera, from the aristocratic precincts of which rigorous restrictions of dress and prohibitive prices excluded the vulgar. The general attitude of society towards the art was essentially that of Lord Chesterfield when he warned his son against a tendency towards being a "fiddler," even in the amateur sense, as wholly unworthy of an English gentleman; or of the poet Byron when he declined to acknowledge the difference " 'twixt Tweedledum and Tweedledee" in the famous epigram generally but erroneously attributed to Swift.

That attitude, one is happy to say, if not altogether extinct, is at least rapidly becoming so. There are still gentlemen of the old school who have a certain pride in confessing their inability to distinguish "God save the Queen" from "Yankee Doodle;" and I remember that at the meeting convened for the discussion of the Royal College of Music, and graciously presided over by the Prince of Wales at St. James's Palace, the speakers, including such men as Mr. Gladstone, the late Lord Iddesleigh, Lord Rosebery, and the late Archbishop of Canterbury, almost without exception prefaced their remarks upon music by saying that they knew nothing whatever about music. But this contemptuous treatment of the art is essentially confined nowadays to official persons, such as provincial mayors, Church and law dignitaries, and the members of the British Government, which, whether Whig or Tory, wastes every year a huge sum of public money on teaching little Board School children to sing "by ear," while it declines to give any support to the higher development of the art, with the exception of a trumpery sum of £500 per annum grudgingly doled out to the Royal Academy.

This stolid obtuseness, formerly so common, can no longer be laid to the charge of intelligent Englishmen; and that this is so, and that musicians are no longer separated from the rest of society by the barrier which of old at fashionable parties took the tangible shape of a cord dividing the professionals from the rest of the company, is in no small measure due to the enlightened encouragement of art and artists by the reigning sovereign. Sir George Macfarren, differing in this from other historians, has more than once expressed an opinion that the decline and fall of English music was not in reality caused by the intolerance of the Puritans and their modern successors, but by the accession of the House of Hanover —a race of aliens with no sympathy for the national development of the art; as if such sympathy could have been expected from the Stuarts, who in their tastes and habits were quite as much foreigners as

George I. and George II. Charles II. had not been many months on the throne when he went out of his way to affront English music. One of the earliest entries in " Pepys's Diary " (October 14, 1660) refers to a visit of Mr. Pepys to Whitehall Chapel, " where one Dr. Croft made an indifferent sermon, and after it an anthem, ill-sung, which made the King laugh." Neither did profane music of English growth find favour with the merry monarch; for, a little more than a month after the last entry (November 20), we find that " at a play the King did put a great affront upon Singleton's musique in bidding them stop, and made the French musique play, which my Lord Sandwich says, do much outdo all ours." On the other hand, when George I. came over to this country he had quarrelled with the great Handel and refused to see him, and it was by no means an easy matter to reconcile the King with his runaway *Kapellmeister*, who had by that time become the darling of the English aristocracy.

Our present Queen has from the first acted upon the wise principle of encouraging the art quite independently of the narrow prejudices of nationality. Every foreign musician of distinction, from Mendelssohn down to Liszt, has met with a gracious reception at Windsor and Buckingham Palace; and before her bereavement withdrew her to a great extent from public amusements, the Queen was a constant frequenter of the Italian Opera. On the other hand, the honour of knighthood has recently been showered upon English musicians with an almost too lavish hand. With the Queen, love of music was an hereditary instinct, further developed by the encouragement and sympathy of her husband, himself an ardent worshipper of the art and a composer of merit. The important part which music played in the home life of this exalted couple is charmingly illustrated in the letters of Mendelssohn, whose genius was acknowledged by them even before the professional critics and the public at large had made up their minds as to his merits. Mendelssohn happened to be present in London at the time of the coronation, and gives a glowing description of that impressive ceremony. He writes, June 28, 1838:

> I have just seen the fair young girl step forth from this gate [the letter contains a sketch of Westminster Abbey as a vignette], and as she, in her mediæval costume, passed down the line of halberdiers, dressed in red, against the venerable grey walls, I could have imagined myself back in the middle ages. It was a very pretty picture, with just a touch of sunlight. May it be a good omen for her reign!"

And again :

> Nothing more brilliant, by the way, could be seen than all the beautiful horses with their rich harness, the carriages and grooms covered with gold embroideries, and the splendidly dressed people inside. All this, too, was encircled by the venerable grey buildings and the crowds of common people under the dull sky, which was only now and then pierced by sunbeams ; at first, indeed, it rained. But when the golden, fairy-like carriage—supported by tritons with

their tridents, and surmounted by the great crown of England— drove up, and the graceful girl was seen bowing right and left; when at that instant the mass of people were completely hidden by their waving handkerchiefs and raised hats, while one roar of cheering almost drowned the peal of the bells, the blare of the trumpets, and thundering of the guns, one had to pinch oneself to make sure that it was not all a dream out of the " Arabian Nights." Then fell a sudden silence, the silence of a church, after the Queen had entered the cathedral.

It was not till four years later that Mendelssohn made the acquaintance of the lady whom he had thus admired at a distance. The passage in which he describes to his mother what one may call a morning's music at Buckingham Palace, is so charming and so pertinent to the subject, that, although long, and quoted before, it deserves insertion here:

Prince Albert had asked me to go to him on Saturday at two o'clock, so that I might try his organ before I left England. I found him alone; and as we were talking away the Queen came in, also alone, in a simple morning dress. She said she was obliged to leave for Claremont in an hour, and then, suddenly interrupting herself, exclaimed, "But goodness! what a confusion!" for the wind had littered the whole room, and even the pedals of the organ (which, by the way, made a very pretty feature in the room), with leaves of music from a large portfolio that lay open. As she spoke, she knelt down and began picking up the music; Prince Albert helped, and I, too, was not idle. Then Prince Albert proceeded to explain the stops to me, and she said that she would meanwhile put things straight. I begged that the Prince would play me something, so that, as I said, I might boast about it in Germany; and he played a chorale by heart, with the pedals, so charmingly and clearly and correctly, that it would have done credit to any professional; and the Queen, having finished her work, came and sat by him and listened, and looked pleased. . . .

Then the young Prince of Gotha came in, and there was more chatting, and the Queen asked if I had written any new songs, and she said she was very fond of singing my published ones. "You should sing one to him," said Prince Albert, and after a little begging she said she would try the "Frühlingslied" in B flat, "if it is still here," she added, "for all my music is packed up for Claremont." Prince Albert went to look for it, but came back saying it was already packed. "But one might perhaps unpack it," said I. "We must send for Lady ——," she said (I did not catch the name). So the bell was rung and the servants were sent after it, but without success; and at last the Queen went herself, and whilst she was gone Prince Albert said to me, "She begs you will accept this present as a remembrance," and gave me a case with a beautiful ring, on which is engraved "V.R., 1842." . . . The Duchess of Kent came in too, and while they were all talking I rummaged about amongst the music, and soon discovered my first set of songs. So of course I begged her to sing one of these, to which she very kindly consented; and which did she choose?— "Schöner und söchner schmückt sich"—sang it quite charmingly, in strict time and tune, and with very good execution. Only in the line "Der Prosa Last und Müh," where it goes down to D and up again by semitones, she sang D sharp each time; and as I gave her the note the first two times, the last time she sang D where it ought to have been D sharp. But with the exception of this little mistake it was really charming, and the last long G, I have never heard better or purer or more natural from any amateur. Then I was obliged to confess that Fanny had written the song (which I found very hard, but pride must have a fall), and to beg her to sing one of my own also. If I would give her plenty of help she would gladly try, she said, and then she sang the Pilgerspruch, "Lass dich nur," really quite faultlessly, and with charming feeling and expression.

In her public encouragement of the art, the Queen has essentially followed that principle of a constitutional sovereign which says, "Le roi ne gouverne pas." She has governed neither concert-room nor theatre, and apart from the expenses of the private band, ably directed by Mr. Cusins, the Royal exchequer has not been drawn upon for any of those contributions which Continental Kings and Kaisers bestow upon their Court theatres. In judging of this fact we should remember, however, that this is the country of self-help, in which art has to take its chance along with other unprotected industries. That it has upon the whole thriven well upon that principle—although a little material support from high quarters might at times have appeared desirable enough—the following remarks will show.

In these remarks, even the briefest summary of the musical events which have happened during the last fifty years will not be attempted. Such a summary would by far exceed the limits of space here at disposal, and would, moreover, only tend to encumber the reader's memory with an endless enumeration of names, and dates, and facts. It will be more to the purpose to sketch in a few words the state of English music in the year 1837, and to indicate in what direction, and by what means, the great change previously alluded to has been effected. The anonymous author of a volume of "Musical Recollections of the Last Half-Century," published in 1872, who, whatever may be thought of his critical faculties, has at least the authority of an eye-witness, speaks of this particular year in a manner which reminds one of the famous Chapter on Snakes in

Iceland. "The concert season of 1837," he writes, "may be dismissed without the slightest reference;" and a little further on he states: "Equally dull and dreary was the operatic season." As regards concerts, however, one important exception should be made—the first performance in London of Mendelssohn's "St. Paul," which was given by the Sacred Harmonic Society, then recently removed to Exeter Hall, on March 7, after having been heard for the first time in England at the Liverpool Festival in the previous October, Sir George Smart acting as conductor. On that occasion the work had been the subject of very divergent comments. One of Mr. Davison's predecessors in the office of musical critic of *The Times* speaks of "St. Paul" as a purely ecclesiastical work, without "fervid bursts of genius or witching graces of melody," and he complains that "Braham had only a single air, or rather he accompanied Linley in a solo," having reference to the famous "Be thou faithful unto death," and its accompaniment for the violoncello obbligato. That nothing else worth mentioning happened in London during the first year of the Queen's reign cannot, of course, be accepted in its literal sense; at the same time, the chances of anything happening were then, comparatively, very limited. The spirit of modern enterprise and competition had not yet entered the quiet realms of music — or at least of orchestral music — for virtuosi were as ambitious, although not quite as numerous, then as they are now.

Virtually, the only stronghold of that form of music was in those days the Philharmonic Society, which still survives. Only a few years before this, it was in so flourishing a condition that, as Spohr writes in his autobiography: "Notwithstanding the high price of admission, the number of subscribers was so great, that many hundreds who had inscribed their names could not obtain seats." New and important works by contemporary musicians were in those days frequently included in the programmes, and in the year 1837 it produced, amongst other things, a symphony by Onslow, and the overture "The Naiads," by Sterndale Bennett—then a young and rising musician, who subsequently became the conductor of the society.

The Antient Concerts were already in a very attenuated condition, although they lingered on for many years afterwards. Their programmes consisted mainly of detached choruses and airs from Handel's oratorios, varied now and then by a song from Purcell or from Cimorosa, or the English Bach, or an overture by Mozart. Even for a complete performance of one of Handel's works this venerable society, founded as early as 1776, had not strength enough left. Its performances were directed (not, of course, conducted) in turns by the Archbishop of York, Royal and other Dukes, and various members of the aristocracy; and the admission was so difficult that ordinary mortals were practically excluded. From 1804 these concerts, previously given in Tottenham Street, and after that at the Concert Room in the Opera House, took place in the Hanover Square Rooms.

It was to make up for the shortcomings of the Antient Concerts that the Sacred Harmonic Society was founded in 1832, and by the time we are speaking of, it had already done excellent work, performing "Israel in Egypt," the "Dettingen Te Deum," "The Messiah," Mozart's "Twelfth Mass," and other works in their complete form. Those who knew the Society and its conductor for many years, Sir Michael Costa, in their old age, could scarcely realise the vast service done by both conjointly to sacred music, which was then, and remains to this day, the most perfect expression of English national feeling in the art of sound. If we look back upon these limited efforts of our grandfathers with something like pity, the feeling is changed to envy when we come to consider the Italian operatic stage of those days, or at least the singers who trod that stage. The season of 1837, as has already been said, was considered by contemporaries an unusually dull and dreary one. Yet we hear of "Grisi's exquisite singing, Lablache's imposing attitudes, and those wondrous high notes of Rubini," as displayed in Costa's *Malek Adhel;* and later on Pasta appears in a selection from *Tancredi* and *Anna Bolena*, given on the same evening of June 29, for the benefit of M. Laporte. All this took place at Her Majesty's Theatre. In the way of journalism, music was represented, apart from the criticisms which appeared cursorily in the daily papers and in *The Athenæum*, by one organ of its own, *The Musical World*, founded in 1836.

Having thus completed the brief summary of things musical in London fifty years ago, it will now be necessary to consider what changes Queen Victoria's reign has brought about. The Antient Concerts have long ago gone the way of all things superannuated, and the Hanover Square Rooms, where they were held, is now the dining-room of a club, with the paintings by Cipriani still remaining in the arched roof. The Philharmonic, as was said before, still exists, but is declined into the vale of years, and shows the signs of senescence. The Sacred Harmonic came to a close five years ago. Its very valuable library is now in the possession of the Royal College of Music. Exeter Hall, which witnessed most of its triumphs, is, as far as music is concerned, mute and inglorious, being given over to May meetings, Young Men's Christian Associations, and the like. As to Italian Opera, very different opinions might be held. Its Juggernaut car has crushed almost every manager approaching it, from the time of Handel to our own. Italy is the land of song no longer. It has only two composers of genius left, one of whom (Verdi) is an old man, albeit still in the full possession of his genius, while the other (Arrigo Boito) is too fastidious or too much occupied in other ways to give a successor to his *Mefistofele*. As to the Italian school of singing, the *bel canto*, it is practically a lost art. Even on so important an occasion as the first performance of Verdi's *Otello* at La Scala, in 1887, Italy was unable to furnish a cast of native singers; and in other countries the so-called Italian stage is invaded by a motley assembly from all quarters of the world, knowing little or nothing of Italian traditions, and pronouncing the language of Dante and Petrarch with multifarious accents, amongst which the *lingua Toscana in bocca Americana* prevails. Mr. Mapleson's last season introduced a score or so of American prima donnas, and perhaps one or two Italian tenors. Italian Opera as a distinct type of art has ceased to exist, and its ruin is due to the so-called " star system," and the caprices and exorbitant pecuniary demands on the part of leading singers which it engenders. Fortunate it is that some of the " stars " are, at least, of such genuine brilliancy as we observe in Madame Patti, Madame Albani, and other excellent artists.

Chronos, in the Greek legend, devours his own children, but luckily their places are filled up again twice and thrice over as soon as they are vacated. Such is the eternal vitality of nature, and of its counterfeit, art. The Antient Concerts are dead, but of new concert institutions, with plenty of life and vigour in them, we have many. Let us first consider orchestral music, which has made enormous strides within the last fifty, or, more properly speaking, within the last twenty years. For the general appreciation of this, the highest form of music in its pure or absolute state, no one has done more in this country than Mr. Manns, the conductor of the Crystal Palace Saturday Concerts. The excellence of these performances is known all the world over, and their programmes comprise almost the entire range of classical and modern music, and bear ample testimony to the catholicity of taste and breadth of knowledge possessed by Mr. Manns and by Sir George Grove, who from the first has been, so to speak, the philosopher and guide of these concerts, and whose analyses of the music performed have largely contributed to their educational value. Additional impetus to orchestral art in this country was given by the advent of Hans Richter, by many considered to be the first of living conductors, and certainly unrivalled in the interpretation of Wagner, excerpts from whose dramatic works, together with Beethoven's symphonies, form the staple of the Richter Concerts. Quite recently the London Symphony Concerts, founded and conducted by Mr. Henschel, have made an important addition to this branch of the art, supplying, at the same time, the long-felt want of high-class orchestral performances in London proper during the winter months. It is especially gratifying to notice that the progress of national taste marked by these facts is not restricted to London. Our large provincial towns are beginning to move. Apart from the great Festivals, which the limits of space make it impossible even to mention by name, some of them have established high-class performances all the year round. Sir Charles Hallé at Manchester, Mr. Stockley at Birmingham, and Mr. Riseley at Bristol, should be mentioned in this connection. The orchestras of these gentlemen consist largely of local musicians, and the flow of healthy decentralisation thus indicated will, it must be hoped, not stop there. Before this reign is over, every great provincial city ought to have an orchestra of its own, and an operatic theatre to boot, even as the small towns of France, Germany, and Italy have such orchestras and theatres, largely supported by municipal liberality.

If orchestral music has been largely developed during the Queen's reign, it may well be said of chamber music, or at least of its public execution, that it took its rise during this reign. The credit is in the first instance due to the late Mr. John Ella. He started, in 1845, a series of morning concerts of instrumental chamber music, which became known as the Musical Union, and were continued by him for thirty-five years, with the result that many works of that class, both classical and modern, and very many of the greatest virtuosi of the day, were for the first time introduced to English amateurs. Mr. Ella, it may be incidentally mentioned, also invented the analytical programmes which have ever since played so important a part in our concert-rooms, although abroad they are as good as unknown.

The Musical Union has ceased to exist; its occupation, indeed, was partly gone when, in the winter of 1858-59, the Monday Popular Concerts were started on the basis of good music at cheap prices. The first performance took place February 14, 1859, being devoted exclusively to the works of Mendelssohn, and including, among other things, an organ performance by Mr. E. Hopkins; a form of art, by-the-bye, which since then has dropped out of the programmes, and might be revived with advantage, provided a better instrument could be found for St. James's Hall. During the first year twelve concerts were given, and the success was such that the director believed the experimental stage to be passed, and announced the Monday Popular Concerts as a permanent establishment. Part of that success was, no doubt, due to the low prices at which high-class music was for the first time offered to the public; for whereas previously reserved seats used to cost fifteen shillings, and unreserved seats ten shillings, the former were here reduced to one-third of that price, and for admittance to the hall the moderate sum of only one shilling was, and is to the present day, chraged

The one-hundredth Popular Concert was given on July 7, 1862, when, according to *The Times,* more than one thousand persons were refused admission for want of space—a statement in itself sufficient to show the broad popular basis on which the concerts were by that time founded. In 1865 the Saturday Afternoon Concerts were added to those given on Monday evenings, and on May 15 of the same year one of the most important events in the history of this institution — the first appearance of Madame Schumann — took place. The programme on that occasion was devoted entirely to the works of her husband, which, in those days, were thought by the public and the press to be the abstruse effusions of the modern spirit, and are now as generally and almost as highly appreciated as those of Beethoven himself. Five years later, in 1870, Madame Norman-Neruda was added to the list of executants, and has remained one of the prime favourites of these and English audiences generally ever since. In the season of 1873–74 more than common attention was paid to contemporary talent, the names of Saint-Saëns, Rubinstein, Rheinberger, Raff, and other then living composers playing a prominent part. The cause of this inroad upon established tradition is partly to be found in the appearance at the piano of Dr. Hans von Bülow, who here, as everywhere else, exercised a beneficial but, so far as the Popular Concerts were concerned, a too passing influence.

There are few names of eminence absent from the list of executants who have appeared on and off. The one-thousandth performance was given on April 4, 1888. Like a mighty tree, the Monday Popular Concerts have thrown out shoots more or less vigorous, which, in the form of annual concerts and series of concerts, come round every season with the regularity of natural phenomena. To mention these, or any of these, this is not the place. What is of more importance is to indicate the growing demand for music of the better class which this increasing supply has created, in accordance with a well-known rule of political economy.

That, together with the good seed thus sown, rank and pernicious weeds are growing apace, is an almost foregone conclusion in a city so vast as London, which contains not one, but five-and-twenty different publics. At St. James's Hall, and at our smaller concert-rooms, to say nothing of innumerable private houses, false sentiment and arrant mediocrity flourish in the shape of the "royalty" song, so called from the blackmail which the singer levies on composer and publisher for advertising, by his performance, what he must know to be the most unqualified trash. The public, as Liberty Wilkes is said to have said, is a goose from which every wise man plucks a feather. This is the same in all countries; still, it must be owned that the goose-like quality in musical matters is proportionately larger in England than elsewhere, or else what could induce even our best singers to minister to it, and to jeopardise their reputation by drawing large profits from the aforesaid abominable system?

To reduce the loud cackle of ganders and geese to a *pianissimo*, to stop the system of blackmailing by enlightening those who are too willing to submit to that tax, will be the task of the large number of music schools and conservatoires which have sprung up during the last few years, hatching our future Beethovens and Marios, and, in a general way, teaching the young idea how to shoot. The educational impetus given to music in this country was largely due to the late Mr. John Hullah, who, in his private, and later on in his official capacity, as Government inspector of schools, did excellent service in diffusing elementary knowledge amongst all classes. In 1840 he went to Paris to study the system inaugurated by Guillaume Louis Bocquillon Wilhem, the founder of popular musical education, and of the important Orphéon movement in France. The principles of Wilhem's method are contained in his "Guide de la Méthode Elémentaire et Analytique de Musique et de Chant," and the same principles Mr. Hullah forthwith proceeded to adapt to English uses. In 1841 he started, at Exeter Hall, classes for the instruction of schoolmasters, and from that modest beginning the vast development of musical training in elementary English schools may be said to have taken its rise.

Mr. Hullah was a firm believer in his own method, and strongly opposed to the so-called Tonic Sol-fa system, which, of late years, has found a vast number of adherents among popular teachers, and the practical results of which cannot be denied, whatever may be thought of its scientific merits. Mr. John Curwen was the founder, in 1853, of the Tonic Sol-fa Association, which has since spread its branches all over England, being especially favoured by the Nonconformists.

Amongst our great music schools only the Royal Academy existed prior to the accession of her present Majesty, having been founded as long ago as 1823. On March 24 of that year the first lesson was given by Mr. Cipriani Potter to Kellow Pye, in the same house in Tenterden Street where the institution still flourishes. As far as outward prosperity and number of pupils are concerned, the Academy has never been in a better condition than at present; and it must be hoped that Mr. A. C. Mackenzie, the new principal, will differ from his predecessor, Sir George Macfarren, by conducting the institution more in accordance with the spirit of the age. That spirit, on the other hand, is, in different ways, represented by two younger institutions: the Royal College of Music, over which Sir George Grove presides, and the Guildhall School of Music, directed by Mr. Weist Hill. The former was opened by the Prince of Wales, who had taken an active interest in the foundation of the school, on

May 7, 1883. Largely by his exertions a sum of money, amounting to over £110,000, had been raised, and the college started with fifty scholarships for tuition, fifteen of which included maintenance, the remainder of the students paying their own fees. The admirable and serious spirit in which the art is taught here has been evinced more than once by the public performances of the pupils. *Ars vera res severa* is evidently the principle of both teachers and taught. The Guildhall School of Music, opened in 1880, which owes its existence entirely to municipal liberality, has long since become self-supporting. In the building erected for it by the Corporation of London on the Victoria Embankment, and inaugurated in December, 1886, it supplies no less than two thousand five hundred pupils with artistic pabulum. The Guildhall School of Music has a special task assigned to it, the task of spreading the taste for the higher forms of music amongst all classes of society. It rests on a popular basis. Its charges are within the means of those even very moderately endowed with the goods of this world, and it accordingly appeals to the people in the broadest sense of the word. It would, of course, be by no means desirable that a tenth or even a hundredth part of the two thousand five hundred pupils should join the professional ranks, although there is no reason why amongst that vast number a few artists of real genius should not be discovered.

To train them up to a certain point all the appliances are at hand. But this is a comparatively remote contingency. The more immediate task of the school is of an educational kind. It should form, in the first instance, good audiences rather than excellent performers. In England such a purification of taste is even more necessary than in other countries, which can look back upon generations of intelligent amateurs. With us the general culture of the art as a national growth is of comparatively recent origin. In consequence, our public labours under the diffidence of inexperience. It is slow to form an opinion of a new work. It prefers to wait and see what the newspapers say the next morning. This is a serious drawback for the art which, like every other modern institution, must draw its strength from the support of an enlightened public opinion. If the Guildhall School will spread that enlightenment amongst ever-widening circles, the trouble and the money spent on it will not have been wasted.

It is curious to observe the comparatively inferior position which the teaching of dramatic music, properly so called, occupies at most of these schools, and the small number of vocalists at all equal to Mr. Sims Reeves, Madame Patey, Mr. Lloyd, and Mr. Santley, which in consequence they have supplied to the stage. There are, indeed, people who believe that our nation has no real taste for the opera, and that the oratorio takes its place as the real expression of our dramatic feeling in music. There are a good many facts which give plausibility to this supposition; the music of Wagner, for example, is highly appreciated in the concert-room, but the attempts that have been made to present his later music-dramas on the stage have been dismal failures in a pecuniary sense. The place of the deceased Sacred Harmonic Society has been taken by numerous choral bodies, amongst which the excellent choir conducted by Mr. Barnby is *facile princeps*. On the other hand, the largest city in the world is able to support an English Opera only during one month, or, at most, six weeks of the year. Of the attempts at establishing English Opera on a permanent basis which were made during the last fifty years, and amongst which the joint enterprise of Miss Louisa Pyne and Mr. W. Harrison was the most important, this is not the place to speak. For the last decade and more the cause of English Opera has rested entirely upon the shoulders of Mr. Carl Rosa. Mr. Rosa at the beginning had not only to get his singers where he could find them in America and England, but he had also to create a *répertoire* for them. That *répertoire* is, of course, not limited to works of English growth, but it includes a considerable portion of them. Mr. Cowen's *Pauline*, Mr. Goring Thomas's *Esmeralda* and *Nadeshda*, Mr. C. V. Stanford's *The Canterbury Pilgrims*, Mr. Mackenzie's *Colomba* and *The Troubadour*, and quite recently Mr. Corder's *Nordisa*, a somewhat unfortunate attempt at reviving the old-fashioned form of English Opera, identified with the poet Bunn and Balfe, have been commissioned and produced with various degrees of success by Mr. Carl Rosa. Of the respective merits of these works it would be inadvisable to speak in a chapter which is a summary of facts and not a criticism; for the same reason the survey of contemporary English art must be limited to an enumeration of some of the most prominent names. From the earlier part of the period here under discussion, the memory of Sterndale Bennett alone survives, and his works are still occasionally heard in our concert-rooms. The veteran composers, Mr. John Barnett and Mr. Charles Salaman, are still amongst us; Mr. Henry Leslie, Mr. Barnby, and Mr. Cusins are well reputed both as composers and conductors. Among the younger men, Mr. John Francis Barnett, Mr. Wingham, Mr. Stanford, Mr. Hubert Parry, Mr. G. H. Lloyd, Mr. Cowen, more successful as a writer of symphonies than as a dramatic composer, Mr. Goring Thomas, Mr. Mackenzie, Mr. Corder, Mr. Hamish MacCunn, a young Scotchman of extraordinary promise, and Sir Arthur Sullivan, so far as outward success is concerned by a long way the first of English composers, may be referred to. Church music, in which England has excelled for many centuries past, has not, of course, been silent during the present reign; and the modern school of English organists, founded by Samuel Wesley, and including such men as Mr. Hopkins, Mr. Best, Dr. Stainer, Dr. Bridge, Mr. Kendrick Pyne, and many others, need not shun comparison with the foreigner.

The question how much of the work done and being done by these and other men will become historical, or whether many or any of their compositions will be remembered fifty years hence, it would be premature to decide. Certain it is that our English school has given signs of various and valuable gifts, and the long mooted discussion as to whether England is or is not a musical country can no longer be said to be *sub judice*. Mr. Cowen's symphonies—particularly the "Scandinavian" and the "Welsh," which have made their way to most European and American concert-rooms—I am prepared to class amongst the best specimens of symphonic writing that could be produced by any living master at home or abroad. Mr. Mackenzie's maiden effort in opera, *Colomba*, showed dramatic qualities of a very high order indeed, as did also the first and the fourth acts of *The Troubadour*, and the so-called dream-scene of the oratorio, "The Rose of Sharon." If the promise here held out has not been altogether fulfilled in other works by Mr. Mackenzie, the fault lies perhaps less with the composer than with the circumstances in which London musicians are compelled to work, surrounded as they are by the turmoil of the largest city in the world, and impelled by competition to produce against time and in excess of the degree of spontaneous inspiration allotted to man. Sir Arthur Sullivan's position in the history of our music is altogether exceptional, if not unique. Royalty has delighted to honour him, and the popular verdict has endorsed the opinion of "society;" yet his time is largely occupied in the production of operettas which, excellent though they are of their kind, are not the class of work upon which great reputations are generally founded. That this gifted composer is capable of treading the higher walks of the art is sufficiently proved by such a work as "The Golden Legend," the opening movement of which, with its novel and poetic effect of cathedral bells made vocal and articulate, in my opinion reveals imaginative qualities of no common order, although the Berlin critics—who, by the way, went into raptures over *The Mikado* —failed to see it. Let us hope that Sir Arthur Sullivan will rise to still higher things in the future. The graceful, although not dramatically very powerful, muse of Mr. Goring Thomas, the author of *Esmeralda* and *Nadeshda*, claims a passing tribute. This composer, nurtured in the traditions of the Opéra Comique, possesses some of the qualities of the French school, and there is no reason why Englishmen should appreciate him less on that account, for art is distinctly an international thing; it is a matter of give and take amongst the peoples of the earth, and any nation that would proudly seclude itself from this continual interchange would, in the words of Othello, cut off

> The fountain from the which my current runs,
> Or else dries up.

In the same sense that Mr. Goring Thomas is influenced by France, Mr. C. Villiers Stanford embodies in his music some of the features of the modern German school; but that foreign example has not altogether extinguished in him the true old English feeling is proved by his choral ballad, "The Revenge," resonant with the roaring of storms and the thunder of guns.

If amongst this array of talent a genius in the proper sense of that much-abused term has not yet made his appearance; if in secular music at least we have not a distinctly national type of art, we may take heart of grace from the thought that the race of great composers is, with one or two exceptions, extinct in other countries as well as our own. It seems as if Nature, after her effort in creating such men as Schumann, Mendelssohn, Liszt, Wagner, Berlioz, and Verdi, had for a time relapsed into a passive stage. The visits, or, as Buddhists would say, the avatars, of genius are like those of angels, few and far between. It is pleasant to think that the next embodiment of this heaven-born spirit is as likely to take place in this as in any other country. Here at least everything is fresh and hopeful, and the English prophet need no longer fear the contempt of his countrymen. In most respects the conditions are more favourable now than at any other period during the long musical epoch, a brief and necessarily very imperfect summary of which has been the object of this sketch.

CHAPTER II.

WAGNER IN ENGLAND.

I.

When Mendelssohn first came to England, in the spring of 1829, he was received with open arms both by artists and by society, and one of the earliest of his charming home letters describes a grand fête at Devonshire House, to which the fortunate youth was invited. Wagner's reception in this country, when he landed at Tower Wharf in the autumn of 1839, was of a very different kind. Neither the Philharmonic directors nor the Duke of Devonshire took the slightest notice of him, for the simple reason, amongst others, that they were not aware of his existence; for Wagner, at the time, was a poor, unknown, and struggling man. The great works destined to revolutionise dramatic music, lay as yet in a dim future not pierced even by his own eye. All that he cared for was to become a famous operatic composer, and to reap the lucrative laurels with which operatic success is crowned in these days, and of which Meyerbeer had earned his fill in Paris.

For that city Wagner was bound when he first approached these shores. He came from Riga in a sailing vessel, having acted as musical director of the theatre of that remote Northern city for some time. Similar appointments at Königsberg and Magdeburg had gone before, and had led to the composition of two operas, one of which, *Das Liebesverbot*, founded upon *Measure for Measure*, was given once at Magdeburg, while the other, entitled *Die Feen*, and developed from a fairy play by Gozzi, never saw the light during the composer's lifetime, although it has quite recently been given at Munich with such success of esteem as is due to the juvenile effort of a great master.

Wagner at last became tired of the narrow misery of provincial theatres; he determined to escape into a higher sphere at any price, and the means he fixed upon for that purpose were thoroughly characteristic of the man. Having read and discerned the operatic potentialities of Lord Lytton's novel, "Rienzi," he sketched the plot and sent it to Scribe for translation, proposing at the same time that the famous librettist should use his influence for the production of the work at the Grand Opera. For, with a view to that theatre the opera had been designed, so as to put any thought of offering it to a German manager out of the question. The result of such an application from a perfect stranger might have been foreseen by any one but the young enthusiast. Scribe, as far as one can tell, did not answer his letter; or, if he did, that answer was the reverse of encouraging. But Wagner, nothing daunted, resolved to see what personal solicitation would do, and he accordingly embarked at Riga in a sailing vessel, accompanied by his wife, *née* Minna Planer, an actress of some talent, to whom he remained fondly attached through good and evil report, and a huge Newfoundland dog, the first probably of a long series of similar monsters without which Wagner did not think life worth living, and one of which lies buried at his feet in the garden of Wahnfried. The direction was in the first instance London, and there the couple arrived after a long and fatiguing voyage. In a note to Mr. Dannreuther's excellent article in Grove's Dictionary, it is stated that they lodged for a night at the "Hoop and Horseshoe," 10, Queen Street, Tower Hill, still existing; then stayed at the King's Arms boarding house, Great Compton Street, Soho; from which place the dog disappeared, and turned up again after a couple of days, to his master's frantic joy. Wagner's accurate memory for localities was puzzled when he wandered about Soho with Mr. Dannreuther in 1877, and failed to find the old house. Mr. J. Cyriax states that the premises have been pulled down.

After a week, they left London for Paris, where Wagner finished his *Rienzi* amongst much misery and tribulation, and where the dog basely deserted him for a wealthy Englishman, if the novelette, "The

End of a Musician in Paris," contains, as is generally supposed, many autobiographical details.

In spite of what has been said, it may well be doubted whether Mendelssohn found at Devonshire House, or even on the trip to the North—which inspired him with his Scotch Symphony, and with the beautiful "Hebrides" overture—more valuable treasures than Wagner brought away from this country, for it was while journeying hither that the idea of *The Flying Dutchman* first dawned upon him, or at least gained realistic and dramatic consistency. The voyage was long and unfavourable; they were driven out of their course, and on one occasion the captain had to seek shelter in a Norwegian port. That it was in such surroundings that Wagner received the vivid impression of the wild atmosphere of storm and sea, and the measured songs of the sailors at their work, which we all know from *The Flying Dutchman*, one might guess, if there were not the master's own testimony on the subject. He was inland born (Leipsic, May 22, 1813), and the terrors and beauties of the sea impressed the young man all the more because they were new to him.

It was yet in another sense that Wagner owed the story of the Flying Dutchman, or at least of its *dénouement*, indirectly to this country. This being one of the very few benefits which he reaped in England, a few words on the subject may not be out of place. Sixteen or seventeen years ago the present writer, then a very young man, made some very minute researches as to the genesis of the Flying Dutchman legend, and embodied them first in *The Academy* newspaper, and afterwards in a book which is not a good book, and, he is happy to think, is now out of print, although at the time it attracted a good deal of attention, and, in a manner, started the literary Wagner movement in England. The result of those investigations may therefore be repeated in outline here.

The story of the Flying Dutchman can be traced back as far as the sixteenth century, and like that of his fellow-sufferer by land, the Wandering Jew, seems to be an outgrowth of the thoroughly revolutionised and exalted state of feeling caused by the two great events of those times—the discovery of a new world by the Spaniards and of a new faith by the Germans. Captain Vanderdecken, as is generally known, tries to double the Cape of Good Hope notwithstanding a heavy gale blowing dead in his teeth, and finding this task too much for him, the obstinate Dutchman swears that he will carry out his purpose, even if he should have to sail till doomsday.

The Evil One, hearing this oath, accepts it in its most literal meaning, and in consequence the unfortunate sailor is doomed to roam for ever and aye on the ocean, far from his wife and his beloved Holland. However, the poets of later ages, pitying the weary wanderer of the main, have tried, in different ways, to release him from this desolate fate. Captain Marryat, in his well-known novel, has not been very fortunate in this respect. Another *dénouement* of the story was invented by Heinrich Heine, and upon this Wagner has avowedly based the poem of his opera.

In Heine's fragmentary story, " The Memoirs of Herr von Schnabelwopski," the hero (who, by-the-bye, shows, only slightly disguised, the characteristic features of the great humourist himself) tells us how, on his passage from Hamburg to Amsterdam, he saw a vessel with blood-red sails—very likely the phantom ship of the Flying Dutchman, whom shortly afterwards he beheld *in ipsissima persona* on the stage of the last-named city. The new feature added to the old story is this: that, instead of an unconditional sentence, Vanderdecken is condemned to wander till doomsday, *unless* he shall have been released by the love of a woman "faithful unto death." The devil, or at least the German devil, being proverbially stupid, does not believe in the virtue of women, and therefore allows the unhappy captain to go ashore once every seven years in order to take a wife. The poor Dutchman has been disappointed in his attempts at finding such a paragon of faithful spouses for many a time, till at last, just after another period of seven years has elapsed, he meets a Scotch (according to Wagner, a Norwegian) merchant, and readily obtains his paternal consent to a proposed marriage with his daughter.

This daughter herself has formed a romantic attachment for the unfortunate sailor, whose story she has heard, and whose picture hangs in her room. When she sees the real Flying Dutchman she recognises him at once by the resemblance with his likeness, and, heroically deciding to share his fate, accepts the offer of his hand. At this moment Schnabelwopski-Heine is, by an unforeseen and indescribable incident, called away from the house, and when he comes back, is just in time to see the Dutchman on board his own ship, which is weighing anchor for another voyage of hopeless despair. He loves his bride, and would save her from the fate that threatens her if she accompanies him; but she, "faithful unto death," ascends a high rock, and throws herself into the waves, by which heroic deed the spell is broken, and the Flying Dutchman, united with his bride, enters the long-closed gates of eternal rest.

Heine pretends, as we have said, to have seen this acted on the Amsterdam stage; this statement, however, he withdrew afterwards, and emphatically claimed as his own the invention of the beautiful and eminently dramatic episode. The former statement was also in so far inaccurate that he never sailed from Hamburg to Holland; his voyage was, on the contrary, directed to London, and here most likely it was also that he made the acquaintance of the Flying Dutchman in a theatrical capacity. The story of a phantom ship seems to have been at that time (1827) to a certain extent popular in England.

A very impressive version of it had appeared in *Blackwood's Magazine* (May, 1821), and this was made the groundwork of a melodramatic production of the late Mr. Fitzball, a prolific playwright of those days.

The piece in question is extremely silly and bad in every respect. Mynheer Vanderdecken here is the slave and ally of some horrid monster of the deep, and his motive in taking a wife is only to increase the number of his victims. In this wicked purpose, however, he does not succeed—the heroine escaping his snares, and marrying (if I remember rightly) a young officer whom she had loved against the will of her father. The piece was running at the Adelphi Theatre about the time of Heine's visit to London, and nothing is more probable than that the German poet, who conscientiously studied the English stage, should have seen it. For the circumstance of the Dutchman's taking a wife, Heine would, in that case, be indebted to Fitzball, in whose piece there also occurs an old picture connected with the story. It would thus be most interesting to note how Heine developed out of these trivial indications his noble idea of the Dutchman's deliverance by the love of a woman. Wagner, on his part, has heightened the dramatic pathos of the fable by making his hero symbolise a profound philosophical idea, thus raising the conception of his character from the sphere of a popular tale into that of artistic significance, out of fancy into imagination. The pitiful figure of Mynheer Vanderdecken becomes an embodiment of life-weariness, longing for death, and forgetfulness of individual pain and struggle, or (which is the same) of existence.

Still, we must acknowledge, it would seem that the modest germs of these grand ideas were furnished to both the German poet and composer by the English playwright.

II.

Between the first and the second visit of Wagner to this country sixteen years elapsed, and during that time a considerable change in his position had of course taken place. It may, indeed, well be doubted whether many people go, during the appointed time of three-score and ten, through half the adventures and perils which fell to the lot of Wagner during the interval referred to. For he was essentially a man of action, who lived both long and much, and who transferred the dramatic impetus of his stage work into his own life. Such a man is likely to suffer much; but, if endowed with supreme genius, his sufferings will, like the actions of the just in the old English poem, "smell sweet, and blossom from the dust." It must be owned that throughout his artistic career life supplied him with plenty of materials for such sufferings and such blossomings. One thinks, with a kind of horror, of what might have happened if his Paris scheme had been successful, if he had been allowed to become, together with Meyerbeer, the fertile provider of grand operas for the international stage. Whether, even in such circumstances, his higher nature would, sooner or later, have recoiled from the flesh-pots is a matter for conjecture. Fortunately, he was exposed to no such temptations; his attempts at placing *Rienzi* or his earlier operas at any of the Paris theatres proved utterly abortive; he had to fathom the lowest depths of musical drudgery to gain a bare living for himself and his wife, and was only saved at the last moment from actual starvation by an unexpected stroke of luck. The score of *Rienzi* was accepted at the Dresden Court Theatre, and the first performance took place, with immense *éclat*, on October 20, 1842; the result soon afterwards being the appointment of the composer as *Kapellmeister* to the Saxon Court. That position Wagner held till the spring of 1849, and three more operas, *The Flying Dutchman*, *Tannhäuser*, and *Lohengrin*, were completed up to that date, and the two former produced at Dresden.

The events which led to Wagner's flight from the Saxon capital are matter of history. The Paris revolution in February, 1848, found its echo in most of the German cities; and Wagner, thoroughly dissatisfied with the humdrum existence of official theatrical life, joined in a movement from which he expected an artistic rather than a political regeneration. What actual part he took in the revolution—whether he ever went beyond inflammatory speeches, and mounted a barricade—has never been sufficiently established. But what he had done was quite enough to bring him within reach of the law, and how real his danger was is sufficiently proved by the fate of his colleague and friend, August Roeckel, the eldest brother of the well-known writer of songs, resident at Bristol, who was captured after the flight in May, and languished in a Saxon prison for thirteen years. The guilt of both men was aggravated by the fact of their being attached to the Saxon Court; and the strong, one is almost inclined to think personal, feeling against Wagner which existed at Dresden, is sufficiently proved by the fact that he also had to wait for twelve years, and employ all manner of princely and other influential intercessors, before the decree of banishment was raised, and he was allowed once more on German ground.

His escape from worse evil he owed, like most other good things which befell him, to the unique friendship of Franz Liszt. That friendship has found a memorial as unique as itself in the correspondence between Wagner and Liszt from 1841 to 1861 which has recently been given to the world by Wagner's widow, Liszt's daughter Cosima, and of which an English version by the present writer appeared in July, 1888. From a letter in this correspondence, and from

Wagner's own statements, it appears that he was staying with Liszt at Weimar early in May, 1849, where he witnessed a rehearsal of *Tannhäuser*, which Liszt had recently put on the Weimar stage. Here, also, he heard that the Saxon police were on his traces, and accordingly borrowed the passport of one of Liszt's friends, Dr. Widmann, by means of which he made his escape to Switzerland. He settled at Zurich, and it was from here that he made his second visit to England.

His thoughts had been directed towards this country for a long time, and it was here that he expected to find sympathy and intelligent acceptance of his ideas after his banishment had precluded him from taking any active part in the musical doings of his own country. To say nothing of an overture on the subject of "Rule Britannia," which belongs to his juvenile period, and the manuscript of which has tracelessly disappeared, there occurs in the correspondence with Liszt, as early as June 5, 1849, reference to a distinct plan of visiting this country. By the advice of Liszt, Wagner had gone once more to Paris with a view of writing a work for the Grand Opera there, and, with his usual sanguine temperament, he saw everything finished in his mind's eye. His subject he intended to lay out for dramatic purposes himself, and then not a hackneyed librettist like Scribe, but a young French poet, with an open mind, was to look after the necessary versification.

"During these slow preparations," he was heard to say, "I shall have to occupy my leisure with London; I am ready to go there as soon as possible to do all in my power for the performance of my works. As to this I expect your friendly command."

Soon afterwards we are informed that he had fixed upon a plan of having *Lohengrin* performed in London, and in English, even before it had been heard in the original. This is the passage alluded to:

> Latterly I have accustomed myself to the notion of giving it to the world at first in a foreign language, and now I take up your own former idea of having it translated into English, so as to make its production in London possible. I am not afraid that this opera would not be understood by the English, and for a slight alteration I should be quite prepared. As yet, however, I do not know a single person in London. . . . Could you manage, dear friend, to write to London and to introduce my undertaking, and could you also let me know to whom to apply further?

Liszt, as usual, was ready with his advice and his help, but he also had few connections in London, and the only person of whom he could think to apply to was Mr. Chorley, the influential critic, who, by the way, took subsequently a most hostile position to Wagner when he came to England. The immediate cause of that visit arose from a different and entirely unexpected quarter. In 1854, the Philharmonic Society, which at that time occupied the leading position amongst musical institutions in England, was undergoing a serious crisis. Sir Michael Costa had resigned his post of conductor, and to find a substitute for him was an extremely difficult task. At a meeting of the directors many names were mentioned; some suggested Lindpaintner, others Berlioz; others insisted upon appointing a musician of English birth, or at least one residing in England. At last M. Sainton, the famous violinist, who, at the age of seventy, still lives amongst us in full possession of his mental and artistic faculties, rose to his feet and named Wagner. He himself had no personal cognisance of Wagner's capacities, neither had any of the other directors, but, as M. Sainton remarked, a man who had been so much abused must have something in him. This sentiment was received with acclamation, and it was unanimously resolved that a leap in the dark should be made.*

* When the above statement, founded upon M. Sainton's relation to me, appeared in *The Quarterly Review*, M. Ferdinand Praeger, one of Wagner's early admirers, addressed a letter to the musical papers, in which the following passages occur: "On the strength of its being a matter of historical interest, I would venture to supply the key to this otherwise too emotional version of the proceedings of the conscientious directors of the Society in question. M. Sainton had a dear old friend, Charles Lüders, an excellent musician, albeit of the so-called old school, and I had the good fortune to be intimate with both. To these friends I had suggested Wagner, of whom neither knew even the existence. . . . When the directors heard that I had proposed to Sainton to name Wagner, I was invited to attend their meeting, where I gave all the information they required. This must have been most satisfactory to them, for I received the voted thanks, and enjoyed the honour of a 'shake hands all round.' The first correspondence concern-

The result of that resolution appears in a letter to Liszt which is not dated, but evidently belongs to the very early part of 1855:

"To-day I was asked, on the part of the Philharmonic Society of London, whether I should be inclined to conduct its concerts this year. I asked in return: (1) Have they got a second conductor for the commonplace things? and (2) Will the orchestra have as many rehearsals as I may consider necessary? If they satisfy me as to all this, shall I accept then? If I could make a little money without disgrace, I should be pleased well enough. Write to me at once what you think of this."

---

ing the matter was between Wagner and myself." Whether it was M. Sainton or M. Praeger from whose head the Wagner idea sprang ready-made, Minerva fashion, those two gentlemen, who are both still amongst us, must settle between themselves. But M. Praeger is quite mistaken when he says: "the first correspondence concerning the matter was between Wagner and myself." Wagner had written to several friends on the subject; he had, indeed, practically accepted the offer of the Philharmonic Society before he even knew M. Praeger's London address. This appears beyond a doubt from a letter dated Zurich, Jan. 6, 1855, and addressed to Herr J. A. Roeckel, which has never been published, and which Mr. Roeckel, of Bristol, the son of Wagner's correspondent, has kindly placed at my disposal. In that letter, Wagner states that he has written to Mr. Hogarth, secretary of the Philharmonic Society, accepting their terms subject to the two conditions mentioned in the text. He then goes on to say: "I have not yet received their answer; but provided I really go to London, I reckon, of course, upon your friendly counsel" (Mr. Roeckel had been in London as Manager of the German Opera). "I have also thought of Ferdinand Praeger, and should be very pleased if he would look after my affairs very carefully; for besides him, I really do not know anybody in London, nor do I intend to make many acquaintances there. At all events, kindly let me have Praeger's address. I scarcely know whether I ought to wish

A little later, Jan. 19, 1855, he writes:

"I am able to-day to send you particulars about London. Mr. Anderson, treasurer of the Philharmonic Society and conductor of the Queen's band, came specially to Zurich to arrange the matter with me. I did not like the idea much, for it is not my vocation to go to London and conduct Philharmonic Concerts, not even for the purpose of producing some of my compositions, as is their wish. On the other hand, I felt distinctly that it was necessary for me to turn my back, once for all, upon every hope and every desire of taking an active part in our own artistic life, and for that reason I accepted the hand held out to me. London is the only place in the world where I can make it possible to produce *Lohengrin* myself, while the kings and princes of Germany have something else to do than grant me my amnesty. It would please me very much if I could induce the English people next year to get up a splendid German Opera with my works, patronised by the Court. I admit that my best introduction for that purpose will be my appointment as conductor of the Philharmonic (the old), and so I consented at last to the sale of myself, although I fetched a very low price—£200 per four months. I shall be in London at the beginning of March to conduct eight concerts, the first of which takes place March 12, and the last, June 25.

---

or not to wish that the matter should come to something." The point is of very little consequence; but when historic statements are made, and authoritatively contradicted, it is as well to be accurate. It may perhaps interest some readers to see the letter addressed by Wagner to the Philharmonic Society, and accepting their appointment subject to the conditions more than once referred to. It is an interesting document, were it only on account of the master's curious French style. It has never been published before, and the original has kindly been placed at my disposal by Mr. W. G. Cusins, in whose possession it is:

MONSIEUR,

En réponse de la demande honorable, que Vous m'addressez au nom de Messieurs les Directeurs de la Société Philharmonique,

Wagner arrived in London late in February, and after staying for a short time at the house of his friend, M. Praeger, at 31, Milton Street, Dorset Square, took rooms at 22, Portland Terrace, Regent's Park. M. Sainton relates that one morning in February, at nine o'clock, a youthful-looking German called on him, in full evening dress, in order to pay him an official visit as one of the Philharmonic directors. At first their intercourse was a little formal, and slightly impeded by Wagner's imperfect knowledge of French; but soon the ice began to thaw, and before an hour was over the two were chatting as if they had known each other for years, and from that moment they were fast friends, and remained, during Wagner's stay in London, inseparable.

de Londres, je me sens obligé de vous faire observer, que avant de me décider finalement, il m'importe de savoir : 1°, s'il-y-aurait un second directeur de Concert, en qualité de "Maître de Concert," pour diriger les pièces des Instrumentistes et Chanteurs concertants, de manière que je n'eusse à diriger que les grandes pièces d'Orchestre et d'Ensemble vocale ? 2°, si l'orchestre serait engagé sur des conditions, qui, par le nombre nécessaire des répétitions, me permettaient de répondre d'un esprit d'exécution, tel qu'il seul me peut décider à m'occuper de manifestations publiques de mon art ?

Attendu que Vous êtes dans le cas, de me contenter parfaitement sur ces deux points, je me déclare prêt à accepter l'engagement de la Société Philharmonique, quand il me sera offert.

Agréez, Monsieur, l'assurance de ma consideration distinguée.

(*Signed*) RICHARD WAGNER.

ZURICH,
   28 *Dez.*, 1854.

Wagner had few other acquaintances in London, and not being able to speak our language, was practically debarred from English society. To that circumstance Wagner's wretched condition while in this country, and the prejudice he conceived and expressed against things English, must be largely attributed. When Heine, who also came to England without proper introductions, and not knowing the language, stood in Cheapside, the crowd of people rushing madly past him reminded him of the fatal crossing of the Beresina Bridge by the fugitive army of Napoleon; so sternly were all the faces set, so madly did they seem to fly from some impending fate. On Wagner the whirl of London life, the intellectual and poetic currents he was unable to fathom, must have made a similar impression. Englishmen were, and had to remain, strangers to him, and strangers appear frequently hostile. There were only two exceptions to this rule, Dr. Wylde, whom Wagner calls "a good man," and Mr. Ellerton. "Recently," he writes to Liszt, May 16, 1855, "a Mr. Ellerton, a rich amateur, has attached himself to me very cordially. He has heard my operas in Germany, and my portrait has been hanging in his room for the last two years. He is the first Englishman I have met who does not care particularly for Mendelssohn—a fine, amiable mind." This Mr. Ellerton, really called John Lodge, for the additional name was assumed at an advanced age for family reasons, had studied in Italy and Germany, and was able to converse with Wagner in his own language, and to enter into his ideas. His not caring much for Mendelssohn must not be accounted bad taste. What Wagner means is probably that Mr. Ellerton did not share the Mendelssohn-worship which in those days was the key-note of English musical taste. What is especially in that gentleman's favour is that he does not seem to have pestered Wagner with his own very numerous compositions. For Mr. Ellerton published more than 120 works, including a "Stabat Mater," a number of symphonies and string quartets, and an opera, *Domenica*, produced at Drury Lane in 1838, of which Mr. Alfred Bunn says that "it won't do; he is a good musician, but not equal to writing for the stage; perhaps he holds himself above it."

Apart from this, his intercourse with Mr. Klindworth, who took long walks with him, and played Liszt's music to him, was of much value to Wagner. Unfortunately that gentleman was in weak health. "Poor Klindworth," he writes, "has been ill all along, and the fact that I could undertake nothing with him has deprived me of a great pleasure. He is better now, but not yet allowed to walk with me. Besides him, my intercourse is limited to Sainton, the leader of the orchestra, who caused my ill-fated appointment here, and a certain Lüders, who lives with him. Both are ardently devoted to me, and do all in their power to make my stay here pleasant. Apart from this, I frequently go to Praeger, a good soul."

The most interesting acquaintance Wagner made in London, and one he highly prized, was that with Berlioz, who was conducting the new Philharmonic Concerts at the time. For him Wagner entertained a very lively admiration, which was not altogether reciprocated by the French composer, who, later on, gloated over the defeat of *Tannhäuser* in Paris in a manner little creditable to his heart. But all this was still in the distant future, and Wagner speaks of his newly-gained friend as one of the few acquisitions of his dreary London days.

"One real gain," he writes to Liszt, "I bring back from England—the cordial and genuine friendship which I feel for Berlioz, and which we have mutually concluded. I heard a concert of the new Philharmonic under his direction, and was, it is true, little edified by his performance of Mozart's G minor Symphony, while the very imperfect execution of his 'Romeo and Juliet' Symphony made me pity him. A few days afterwards we two were the only guests at Sainton's table. He was lively, and the progress in French which I have made in London permitted me to discuss with him for five hours all the problems of art, philosophy, and life, in a most fascinating conversation. In that manner I gained a deep sympathy for my new friend; he appeared to me quite different from what he had done before. We discovered suddenly that we were, in reality, fellow-sufferers, and I thought upon the whole I was happier than Berlioz. After my last concert he and the other few friends I have in London called upon me; his wife also came. We remained together till three o'clock in the morning, and took leave with the warmest embraces."

Berlioz, on his part, gives a description of this London episode to Liszt, in which he says: "Wagner is splendid in his ardour, and I confess that even his violence delights me. He has something singularly attractive for me, and if we both have asperities, those asperities dovetail with each other," accompanying the last remark by an indented line, the angles of which run in parallels.

Wagner's professional prospects appeared at first very bright. M. Sainton gives an interesting description of the first rehearsal, at which Wagner conducted the Heroic Symphony of Beethoven without book—at that time an almost unprecedented feat of memory, although since then Herr Richter and other conductors have imitated it. The orchestra and the few persons present were at once astonished and delighted at the new reading given to the familiar work, the delicacy of the *nuances* insisted upon, the intelligence and fire with which the melodies were phrased. After the rehearsal the musicians broke out into a storm of applause such as has been seldom heard in an English concert-room.

Wagner himself was extremely pleased with his reception, as the following extracts will show:—

> After the first rehearsal, the directors of the Philharmonic were so delighted and full of hope that they insisted on my performing some of my compositions at the very next concert. I had to yield, and chose the pieces from *Lohengrin*. . . . The orchestra, which has taken a great liking to me, is very efficient, and possesses great skill and fairly quick intelligence; but it is quite spoilt as regards expression—there is no *piano*, no *nuance*. It was astonished and delighted at my way of doing things. With two further rehearsals I hope to put it tolerably in order. But then this hope and my intercourse with the orchestra are all that attract me here; beyond this all is indifferent and disgusting to me. The public, however, have distinguished me very much, both in receiving me and even more at the close. Curious to me was the confession of some Mendelssohnians that they had never heard and understood the overture to the *Hebrides* as well as under my direction.

The first Philharmonic Concert took place on March 12. On the next day, most of the daily papers came out with a shower of abuse, which was echoed in the weeklies, notably in *The Athenæum*, and continued without abatement during the entire stay of Wagner in London. M. Sainton relates that, at the next rehearsal, when Wagner entered the orchestra, not a hand was raised to welcome him, the musicians receiving him with absolute silence. He himself attributes this change of attitude to the influence of the press, while Wagner discovers in it the influence of Costa, "the real master and despot of the musicians, who can dismiss and appoint them according to his will." Probably both were right. Wagner, although, we have seen, a true and warm-hearted friend, was little conciliatory in his manner to strangers; and the asperities, of which Berlioz speaks, naturally roused the indignation of those who came into contact with them. He was well known to be no admirer of Italian Opera; and the Italian faction, with Costa at their head, naturally hated him. What was worse, he had written a very ill-judged pamphlet against the Jews, in which Mendelssohn and Meyerbeer were severely criticised, although by no means vulgarly abused. Meyerbeer's influence was far-reaching, and Mendelssohn was at the time the idol of the English public. We have been informed on the best authority that Wagner, when he had to conduct a work by Mendelssohn, deliberately and slowly put on a pair of white kid gloves to indicate the formal, or, one might say, fashionable character of the music; and this piece of bad taste naturally roused the ire of Mendelssohn's admirers in the press and elsewhere. As is usual in such cases, both sides were to blame. But at the same time it remains a matter of regret that the influence which a man of Wagner's genius and high artistic aims might have had on English music, was thus almost literally "snuffed out by an article."

That article, perhaps I should say that series of articles, appeared in *The Times* newspaper. Mr. J. W. Davison, at that time the musical representative of the great English organ, was, like all good critics, not a mere reasoner, but a man of imagination, and, like all imaginative men, a good hater as well as a good lover. To dislike Wagner he had more than one reason, amongst which his passion for Mendelssohn was the first and foremost. Mendelssohn to him was not only the dearest of friends, but the greatest of modern musicians, and any one who had spoken of Mendelssohn with the disrespect that Wagner had shown, was, *à priori*, an object of aversion. In such circumstances, calm criticism was a matter of extreme difficulty, almost of impossibility. One should bear this in mind while reading the following extracts. I need not say that they are quoted with no desire of disparaging the memory of a dear friend and colleague, whose vast knowledge of the literature of music and keen appreciation of its beauties made him an excellent judge, when his judgment was not, as in the present instance, blinded by prejudice. That Mr. Davison, in his treatment of Wagner, both as a conductor and composer, was egregiously mistaken, few impartial judges will deny nowadays. But that mistake did, upon the whole, credit to his heart; and what writer on music or on art is there who can open old volumes of his writings without a certain tremor? Critics are, after all, the children of their time, a little raised perhaps by experience and study above the level of current opinion, but still far from infallible.

The first Philharmonic Concert of the season, as has been said, took place on March 12, and *The Times* of the 14th remarks that the Philharmonic Society had not loved Costa wisely, but too well; and that the *bâton* had been offered to Berlioz, who was already engaged for the new Philharmonic Concerts. Nothing was known of Wagner's music in this country except the Overture to *Tannhäuser*, which was at the best but a commonplace display of noise and extravagance. "No other musician," *The Times* goes on to say, "foreign or English, capable of beating time to the symphonies of Mozart and Beethoven being available within a distance of a thousand miles and more, one of the directors was dispatched to Zurich. . . . Wagner was chosen as being probably the very opposite of the Italian conductor." Then follow some disparaging remarks on Wagner's career and opinions:

Haydn's Symphony No. 7 was executed with amazing spirit. Such a familiar work, however, in the hands of such a company of players, would fare well even without a conductor. It was in the (dramatic) concerto by Spohr, magnificently played by Ernst, the ("Isles of Fingal") overture of Mendelssohn, and the ("Eroica") symphony of Beethoven that the qualities of the new director were put to the test. The result, on the whole, was by no means satisfactory; but this may be accounted for in more ways than one. Herr Wagner's method of using the *bâton* (like that of some other German musicians) must be very perplexing at first to those unacquainted with it, and the confusion between the up and down beat, which he appears to employ indiscriminately (so unlike the clear and decided measure of his predecessor), requires a long time to get accustomed to. Moreover, Herr Wagner conducts without a score before him, which says more, we think, for his memory than for his judgment. Such precedents are dangerous. Supposing a leading instrument, entrusted with an important passage, were to be found "napping" (which is possible), and that Herr Wagner's memory should fail him at a pinch (which is possible—for if Homer nods, why not the author of *Lohengrin?*), what would be the consequence? A dead standstill—nothing less. Herr Wagner, however, did not "nod" last night, but exhibited unabated energy and fire; and though his readings are in many places new and strange, his changes perpetual and fidgety, his indications of *tempo* sometimes quicker (as in the first movement of the "Eroica" and the coda of the "Isles"), sometimes slower (as in Beethoven's slow movement and the opening of Mendelssohn's overture) than we have been accustomed to; and although, for these and other reasons too numerous to mention, the band did not go so smoothly or pointedly, or generally so well as we have been accustomed to, we must decline at present to offer any positive opinion about his merits as a *chef d'orchestre*.

The second concert, at which Beethoven's 9th Symphony and extracts from *Lohengrin* were performed, and for which, as Wagner remarks, with ironic emphasis, the directors actually granted him *two* rehearsals, was, curiously enough, not noticed in *The Times* at all, neither was that of April 16th.

With regard to the fourth concert, of April 30, we read as follows:

Wagner's mode of conducting does not seem to win upon the orchestra under his direction, nor his interpretations of the great composers to invite the adherence of connoisseurs. Weber's overture was encored. It was much too fast in some places . . . . and was hardly redeemed by the impetuous enthusiasm imparted to certain points. Beethoven's Symphony No. 7 showed the same discrepancies . . . . etc., etc.

Of the fifth concert, of May 14, similar complaints are made with regard to Mozart's Symphony in E flat, but—

The "Pastoral Symphony" was a great deal better, and the conductor seemed more at home. But even in this liberties were taken which, had the effect been good, might have passed unnoticed, but, since it was not good, only elicited a protest. . . . Of the overture to *Tannhäuser* we have already spoken, and the execution last night gave us no cause to modify our first impression. A more inflated display of extravagance and noise has rarely been submitted to an audience; and it was a pity to hear so magnificent an orchestra engaged in almost fruitless attempts at accomplishing things which, even if really practicable, would lead to nothing. The quaint and characteristic overture to *Preciosa* was played with great spirit, and brought the concert to an end with *éclat*. . . .

At the concert of May 28, as even *The Times* was obliged to admit, the performance of the G minor Symphony by Cipriani Potter was directed—

With evident good-will. . . . The overture to *Leonora*, although the opening slow movement was a little mysterious, went with more decision than anything we have hitherto heard played under Herr Wagner's *bâton*. Mendelssohn's (A minor) symphony was by no means so happy. The *tempi* were all wrong, excepting in the slow movement. . . . It was listened to with apathy. Spohr's overture ("Berg-geist") was well executed.

Concert of June 11; *The Times* says:

Herr Wagner, to his credit be it said, took as much pains with Macfarren's "Chevy Chase," as he had done with Potter's Symphony at the sixth concert. Of the two symphonies we may at once say that Beethoven's (No. 8) went the best. The only fault we could find was with the extreme slowness of the minuet. . . .

In the trio, where the cello obbligato has of late years been allotted to all the celli, Herr Wagner maintained the original design of the composer, and gave it to the principal alone. Strange to say, however, in this instance we prefer the innovation to the first intention. Mozart's "Jupiter" Symphony was, to speak mildly, sacrificed to the whims and caprices of the conductor.

The Times, on the subject of the eighth and last concert of "one of the most unprosperous seasons," has much to say.

Spohr's third symphony and Beethoven's fourth were not well played, indeed, it would scarcely be possible for a symphony so well known as Beethoven's B flat to go worse. . . . The engagement of Herr Wagner has not proved fortunate. No foreign conductor ever came with such extraordinary pretensions and produced so unfavourable an impression. We should not quarrel with Herr Wagner's "new readings," although we agree with few of them, if he could render them intelligible to his orchestra. But this he has failed to do, and the result has been a series of performances unparalleled for inefficiency. The fact is that the author of *Lohengrin* knows better how to theorise fancifully than to reduce his theories to practice. His conducting shows as great a lack of the requisite science as his music. . . . Herr Wagner has cut a sorry figure in this country, where plain common sense goes for something. . . . We believe him to be a very clever man, one of the most subtle and specious indeed of a race of modern German system-makers; but his works present irrefutable proofs that his organisation is *not* musical, and a musician, like a poet, is born, not made. Another such set of concerts would go far to annihilate the Philharmonic Society.

The historic importance of this indictment, which deserved quotation as an authentic expression of critical opinion of the time, is increased by the fact that it seems to have served as a watchword to the remainder of the press. The opinion of *The Times* was echoed by the other papers, as far as I have thought it necessary to consult them; with one notable exception, however. This was *The Daily News*, at that time musically represented by Mr. George Hogarth, Dickens's father-in-law. That gentleman took Wagner's part with a warmth and ability highly creditable to his critical judgment. One extract with regard to the opening concert must here suffice. If ever doctors differed, it was on this occasion.

Mr. Hogarth wrote in *The Daily News:*

<blockquote>
Haydn's charming symphony was certainly never more delightfully played. The andante was taken a little slower than usual here, and we thought that the effect of the movement was thereby enhanced. . . . The orchestra in accompanying achieved the great desideratum, a true *piano*. Beethoven's "Eroica" was magnificently executed from beginning to end; we never heard the band play more evidently *con amore*, nor ever observed a better understanding or more complete sympathy between them and the conductor, and we felt as much gratified as surprised that such a result should have been effected by a single rehearsal. Whatever differences and controversies may exist as to the doctrines and tenets of the musical school, to which Herr Wagner is said to belong, and as to his own character as a composer, disputes into which we do not enter because we are as yet unacquainted with their merits—on one point he has left no room for question—his consummate excellence as an orchestral chief.
</blockquote>

It is curious to note that the tone adopted by Mr. Hogarth in his history of the Philharmonic Society, published in 1862, is entirely different from these extracts, which were written under the immediate impression of a great event. "During the season of 1855," we are told there, "Herr Wagner, though he discharged his duties with great care and assiduity, was unable to gain the confidence of the orchestra or the favour of the public. The season altogether was neither pleasant nor successful, and at its close, Wagner hastened to take his departure from England."

As regards the last sentence, I have been assured by Mr. W. G. Cusins, Master of the Queen's Music, and for a number of years conductor of the Philharmonic Society, that, in spite of the attacks of the press, the Philharmonic season of 1855 was, in a pecuniary sense, an extremely successful one. The public were eager to see the man who excited such ire in celestial bosoms, and many of those who came to scoff remained to admire. The final concert, indeed, took the form of an absolute triumph for the much maligned conductor, and the scene, as described by Wagner, and fully endorsed by a remark in *The Daily News*, is well worth quotation.

At the last concert (Wagner writes), the public and the orchestra roused themselves to a demonstration against the London critics. I have always been told that my audiences were very much in my favour, and of the orchestra I could see that it was always most willing to follow my intentions as far as bad habits and want of time would allow. But I soon saw that the public received impressions slowly and with difficulty, and was unable to distinguish the genuine from the spurious, trivial pedantry from sterling worth, while the orchestra—out of regard for its real master and despot Costa, who can dismiss and appoint the musicians according to his will—always limited its applause to the smallest and least compromising measure. This time, at the leave-taking, it broke through all restraint. The musicians rose solemnly, and, together with the whole thickly crowded hall, began a storm of applause so continuous that I really felt awkward. After that the band crowded round me to shake hands, and even some ladies and gentlemen of the public held out their hands to me, which I had to press warmly. In this manner my absurd London expedition finally took the character of a triumph for me, and I was pleased at least to observe the independence of the public which this time it showed towards the critics.

How much of this "ovation" was due to genuine admiration of Wagner's work, how much to the genuinely English desire of doing kindness to an injured man, may be open to doubt.

There were, however, two very distinguished persons who treated Wagner and Wagner's art in a manner which almost moved him to tears. "You have probably heard," he writes to Liszt, "how charmingly Queen Victoria behaved to me. She attended the seventh concert with Prince Albert, and as they wanted to hear something of mine, I had the *Tannhäuser* overture repeated, which helped me to a little external *amende*. I really seemed to have pleased the Queen. In a conversation I had with her, by desire, after the first part of the concert, she was so kind that I was really quite touched. These two were the first people in England who dared to speak in my favour openly and undisguisedly, and if you consider that they had to deal with a political outlaw, charged with high treason and 'wanted' by the police, you will think it natural that I am sincerely grateful to both."

In spite of these few bright points, Wagner's days in London were amongst the unhappiest of his eventful career, but it is interesting to observe how, even in such circumstances, he was able to forget external troubles over a subject that really laid hold of his mind. The instrumentation of *Die Walküre* was, for the greater part, finished at Portland Terrace, and the masterly exposition of Buddhism as distinguished from the asceticism of Dante's "Divina Commedia," in a letter to Liszt, is dated from London.

Wagner left England immediately after the last Philharmonic Concert, and arrived in Zurich on June 30, glad to be home again, and more eager than ever for his work, which he had given up almost entirely during the latter days of his London purgatory. An offer seems to have been made to him to conduct the new Philharmonic Concerts of 1856, but this he declined to do. The old Philharmonic directors never proposed to renew this engagement.

Before leaving this part of the subject, we must lay before our readers two interesting letters, for which we are indebted to their recipient, M. Prosper Sainton, and which show Wagner in a most amiable light— full of gratitude for the kindness that had been shown to him, looking back upon his London troubles with a certain humour, remembering old friends by their nicknames, and old stories and old jokes. I should add, by way of commentary, that the *chagrins et désagréments* mentioned in the letter refer to the secession of M. Sainton from the Philharmonic Society, which Wagner erroneously attributes to the friendship shown to him by that gentleman. The Mr. Bumpus, about whose welfare he so anxiously inquires, is the bookseller in Oxford Street, whom Wagner, of course, had never met, but whose thoroughly insular name amused him very much. The peculiar French in which these letters are written adds to their charm.

ZURICH, 19 *December*, '55.

CHER PROSPÈRE !—C'est aujourd'hui que je viens de quitter le lit de malade, que j'ai gardé pendant deux mois à l'exception de peu de jours. C'était—je crois—la maladie de Londres, longtemps cachée, qui est éclatée enfin, pour me rappeler ce que je dois à toi et à tes soins bien amicaux, sans lesquels j'aurais probablement trouvé ma mort—là d'où je n'ai remporté maintenant qu'une certaine collection de rhumes et de catarrhs latents qui viennent de sortir enfin de leur cage. Les vapeurs de Londres s'ayant enfuies finalement, tant de mon corps que de mon esprit, ma première occupation est de ramasser tout le français que je puisse encore trouver dans ces coins de mon pauvre cerveau, où—d'après la doctrine du professeur Praeger—naissent nos facultés linguistiques ; car je me sens vraiment agité et pressé à t'écrire, et à te dire, que je t'aime toujours encore, et qu'un de mes plus doux souvenirs, c'est ta connaissance et ton amitié. Le croieras-tu ?—

Pourtant je ne veux pas te cacher que ces souvenirs sont accompagnés par des regrets :—je sens que mon amitié t'a beaucoup coûté. Si je pouvais effacer quelque chose de ma conduite passée, ce seraient ces plaintes et temoignages de mécontentement que je t'ai donnés tant de fois à entendre, en récompense de ta meilleur volonté, et, surtout, des chagrins et des désagréments assez affligeants, que tu devais essuyer alors toi-même, à cause de moi. . . . Te voilà maintenant payé comme tu le meritais. Et qu'est-ce que tu as gagné en échange de ce que tu as perdu? Hélas! un triste don, mon amitié, et le souvenir d'un homme mélancolique, fort souvent insupportable qui mangeait tes dîners et attaquait ta meilleure humeur par son français horrible! Voilà ta récompense! Et moi? ne devrais-je pas être mortifié par l'idée de t'avoir attiré tout cela sans te pouvoir restituer la moindre part de ce que tu as perdu à cause de moi? Tout ce qui me console un peu, c'est la leçon que tu as reçue, et qui t'aura appris de ne t'occuper jamais, quant à l'art que des hommes d'une trempe bien différente de la mienne. Mais comme je suis le plus âgé je te donne encore un conseil un peu grec:

Μῆνιν ἄειδε Θεά Πηληϊάδεω 'Αχιλῆος.

Tu me comprendras!

Eh bien! Il faut maintenant bien faire bonne mine à mauvais jeu, c'est pour cela que je te prie de demander à Lüders ce que fait Bumpus? S'il m'en peut donner de bonnes nouvelles, cela me consolera et touchera profondément. J'espère qu'il va bien? Et la sallade d'homard, et les bouteilles de soda-water, qui étaient toujours si affreuses pour vous deux à voir? Et Charlemagne?— Il Trovatore, et les amis guerriers d'Alira.

À la verité, je t'assure que je porte un grand et vif désir d'avoir des nouvelles de votre part, mais bien larges—très larges! Entends-tu bien? Ou m'en veux-tu à présent, puisque tu as appris que ma connaissance t'a porté de malheur? Je n'y crois pas; car je sais que tu es, avant tout, excellent garçon, cœur généreux. . . .

Allons donc! Gardon notre amitié qui m'est à moi précieux comme un sourire inattendu du destin. Espérons nous revoir un jour pour continuer ce que n'a que commencé, et bravons les canailles!

Adieu, mon très cher Prospère! Mille saluts à Lüders et à la maison Praeger, mes parents! Je te remericie encore de tout mon cœur pourtant de bien dont tu m'as comblé, et suis persuadé de ce que je n'en perdrais jamais le souvenir.

Ton tout dévoué frère et ami,
RICHARD WAGNER.

A second letter, addressed to M. Sainton, is dated Bayreuth, 1875. At that time Wagner was in the zenith of his fame, and just preparing a performance of his *Nibelungen Ring* at the Bayreuth Theatre, erected for him by the liberality of his admirers, and of the King of Bavaria. But he had not forgotten his old London friends, and a letter from M. Sainton, which reached him in the middle of his excitement, immediately elicited the following reply:

MON CHER SAINTON,—Tu n'avais pas besoin de me rappeler ton souvenir. J'ai dicté à ma femme ma vie entière; elle la voulait savoir au fond. Cela est écrit et sera legué à mon fils, pour le faire paraître après ma mort. Et quoi? Vous vous figurez de ne pas figurer dans cette vie? Diable! No. 8, Hind Street. Et Lüders? Toute votre histoire à vous deux est déposée dans ce manuscrit depuis Helsingfors jusqu'à Toulouse (en passant Hambourg). Et puis Londres?—Charlemagne? Où as-tu le sens, mon cher?

Eh bien! Rapelle-toi bientôt à ce qu'existe encore un certain chef-d'orchestre de l'annienne Philharmonie (pensionné?) à Bayreuth (en Bavière, non Syrie!).

Prends un beaujour ta chère femme, charge Lüders sur tes épaules, monte un bon *cab* à l'heure, et arrive à juste temps à Wahnfried; à une heure nous dînons (!!) souper à sept heure du soir.

Et maintenant, trève aux Lohengrins à Londres, ç'a m'a coste!—Mais si tu veux, apporte ton violon avec toi, et puis les Nibelungen feront les honneurs à vous tous.

Force de salutations cordiales de la part de ton ancien ami,

RICHARD WAGNER.

BAYREUTH, 4 *Juin*, 1875.

III.

Twenty-two years elapsed after Wagner's hurried departure before he again set foot on English ground.

Once more the interval had wrought an important change, both in his position in the art world and in musical things in England. In 1877, Wagner was in the zenith of his fame; the first of the Bayreuth performances had been given in the previous year, and had placed the master, as he said in his speech after the curtain had closed on the last of the Nibelungen dramas, in a position which before him no artist had occupied. A theatre had been built for the performances of his own works, and Bayreuth promised to become the artistic Mecca, not only of the disciples of a certain school, but of all who cared for ideal aspirations in art. Only one thing had been wanting—pecuniary success. In spite of all that the Wagner societies and the King of Bavaria had done, in spite also of the large support of outside amateurs, including many Englishmen and Americans, the enormous expenses of the undertaking had not been covered; and it was partly to make up the deficit that Wagner undertook once more to cross the British Channel. The first idea of giving a series of monster concerts at the Albert Hall seems to have originated with Herr Wilhelmj, the famous violinist, who had led the Bayreuth orchestra in splendid style. But the enterprise itself was due to Messrs. Hodge & Essex, of Argyll Street. Six concerts were accordingly advertised, to consist of excerpts from Wagner's works, beginning with *Rienzi*, and ending with the *Götterdämmerung*. *Parsifal* had not yet been written in those days, although the poem was in existence, and was read by the master to a small circle of friends in London. Many of the Bayreuth artists, including Madame Materna, were to take part in the performances, and a colossal orchestra of 170 performers had been engaged. Wagner himself had undertaken to conduct the first part of each concert, while Hans Richter, also with Bayreuth laurels fresh upon his brow, was to direct the second. Mr. Edward Dannreuther had superintended the rehearsals.

Wagner took a great interest in this matter; he was evidently eager that Englishmen should receive as correct and comprehensive a view of his art as could be obtained apart from the stage, and he had for that purpose prepared the programmes with great care. The originals of these programmes, drawn up and the greater part of the verses written in his own neat handwriting, are now in my possession.

Before speaking in detail of the Wagner Festival of 1877, it will be well to say a few words as to the progress which the music of the future had in the meantime made in England. There is a certain poetic justice in the fact that, as Wagner in 1855 had been, as I said before, snuffed out by an article, so the way for his triumphant return in 1877 was paved by a literary movement which was started when only a single opera of his had been performed in this country, and when little more than his name was known to the general public. Of that movement it beseems the present writer to speak with modesty and a certain reluctance, for the reason that it was he who began it. Wagner's pamphlet on Beethoven, written in connection with the centenary of the master's birth, was published in December, 1870; and that profound and brilliant *exposé* I took for the subject of a long and comprehensive article in the *Academy* newspaper, which was soon afterwards enlarged into an essay in *The Fortnightly Review*, and finally developed in the volume, "Richard Wagner and the Music of the Future," which, although imperfect enough as a literary effort, served at least to place Wagner's theory, and the embodiment that theory had found in his artwork, before English readers. A series of excellent essays published by Mr. Dannreuther in *The Monthly Musical Record* and subsequently collected in a brochure, tended in the same direction, although appealing, in its original form of publication, to a more limited circle. The interest attracted by these writings was very general, and a perfect flood of criticisms and articles appeared in various newspapers and reviews. Most of these were distinctly hostile, but the controversy thus set going served at least to make impartial persons anxious to become better acquainted with the style of music which gave rise to so many divergent comments.

Wagner watched these proceedings with a lively interest. In spite of the evil reception he had met with in this country, he never lost his faith in the musical susceptibility of the English nation, closely allied as it was to his own; and any sign of sympathy that came to him from this country he always welcomed with special warmth. To this feeling the exaggerated terms of acknowledgment in which Wagner spoke of these literary contributions are no doubt attributable; he remembered English press utterances of sixteen years ago, and the contrast struck him accordingly. Alluding apparently to some scheme, of the exact nature of which I am ignorant, he wrote in a letter dated Lucerne, April 14, 1871: "You will soon have an opportunity of seeing that I do not undervalue the sympathy of foreign countries with the new phase of the development of the German spirit. In the meanwhile such utterances as yours are in the highest degree welcome to me!" Referring to the article in *The Fortnightly Review*, Madame Wagner wrote later on: "My husband does not read English very fluently, but what I have communicated to him of your essay has highly interested and pleased him. Years ago, *The Westminster Review* published an article entitled 'Lyric Feuds,' which deals with the Wagner question at some length. This article is probably the only thing that had preceded yours in the English language." It appeared, I have since taken the trouble to ascertain, in July, 1867, and considering the time at which it was written, is a distinctly laudable effort. The "Lyric Feuds" alluded to are those between Handel and Buononcini, and Gluck and Piccinni in Paris. To the Wagner question seventeen pages are devoted. The writer evidently has very little knowledge of Wagner's music, and speaks of the "new 'school' of Wagner and Schumann;" but he is much impressed with the beauty of the master's literary style as displayed in the French translation of his four operatic poems, and the letter to M. Villot, also written in French.

To return once more to the Wagner movement in England, brief reference should be made to the foundation of the first Wagner Society in 1873, which had a president in the person of the Earl of Crawford and Balcarres, at that time Lord Lindsay, and an influential council, but existed essentially, like Schumann's Davidsbund, in the head of its founder and musical director, Mr. Edward Dannreuther, to whom the present writer served as humble literary adviser and amanuensis. Two concerts were given at the Hanover Square Rooms, on February 19 and May 9, 1873, and the pecuniary result was so favourable that a respectable sum was remitted to the Bayreuth Theatre Fund. In the late autumn of 1873, and the spring of the following year, six further concerts were given; but these were less successful, owing, perhaps, to the fact that the programmes included a great deal of other music than Wagner's, and the enterprise, therefore, was allowed to drop. An interesting incident in the lives of the conductor and the honorary secretary of the old Wagner Society was their visit in an official capacity at Bayreuth, when the foundation stone of the Wagner Theatre was laid on May 22, 1872. They both made Wagner's personal acquaintance on that occasion, and witnessed a performance of the "Kaisermarsch" and Beethoven's Ninth Symphony, under Wagner's direction. The event, perhaps the most memorable in his musical life, was thus recorded by the present writer:

It is difficult to say what are the mysterious conditions of musical leadership; they are certainly nearest akin to the qualities of a great military commander; and one can only agree with good old Emperor William, who, himself entirely innocent of musical knowledge, said, after Wagner's late performance of Beethoven's C minor Symphony at Berlin, in his homely way, "Now you see what a good general can do with his army."

It is indeed one of the most interesting sights to see the immediate *rapport* established between Wagner and his orchestra as soon as he raises his *bâton*. Each individual member, from the first violinist to the last drummer, is equally under the influence of a great personal fascination, which seems to have much in common with the effects of animal magnetism. Every eye is turned towards the master; and it appears as if the musicians derived the notes they play, not from the books on their desks, but from Wagner's glances and movements. I remember reading in Heine a description of Paganini's playing the violin, and how every one in the audience felt as if the virtuoso was looking at and performing for him or her individually. A gun aimed in the direction of many different persons is said to produce a similar illusory effect; and several artists in Wagner's orchestra and chorus assured me that they felt the fascinating spell of the conductor's eye, looking at them during the whole performance. Wagner, in common life, is of a rather reserved and extremely gentlemanly deportment; but as soon as he faces his band a kind of demon seems to take possession of him. He storms, hisses, stamps his foot on the ground, and performs the most wonderful gyratory movements with his arms; and woe to the wretch who wounds his keen ear with a false note! At other times, when the musical waves run smoothly, Wagner ceases almost entirely to beat the time, and a most winning smile is the doubly-appreciated reward of his musicians for a particularly well-executed passage.

The practical results of the literary campaign, apart from the concerts of the Wagner Society, did not amount to very much. *The Flying Dutchman* had already been performed before its commencement in the autumn of 1870, at Drury Lane Theatre, when Mr. Santley was the Dutchman, and Madame Ilma di Murska an excellent Senta. Signor Arditi, who conducted, did his best to inspire chorus and orchestra with his own love for this weird sea music, and the general performance was all that could be expected in the circumstances; and so, indeed, was the appreciation of an unsophisticated audience. Unfortunately the work had been delayed until the fag end of the season, and disappeared again from the *répertoire* for many years. In 1875, *Lohengrin*, and in 1876, *Tannhäuser*, saw the light of the Anglo-Italian stage; but in spite of the excellence of Madame Nilsson, Madame Albani, and other artists, the general spirit of these renderings was the antipodes of what Wagner had intended. The routine of conventional opera proved too much for the new spirit here at work; and it is no secret that Wagner considered the performance of *Tannhäuser* at Covent Garden the worst he had ever seen for *ensemble*, while acknowledging, at the same time, the vocal achievements of individual singers.

Wagner arrived in London on April 30, 1877, and took up his residence with his friend, Mr. Edward Dannreuther, at 12, Orme Square. Perhaps it would have been better for the external success of his enterprise had he lived in great state at Claridge's Hotel, like a prince and ruler of men as he was; but in spite of what his enemies said of his love of luxury, and in spite of his undoubted predilection for beautiful things and beautiful clothes on æsthetic grounds, his personal habits were extremely simple, and he found in the house and in the family circle of Mr. Dannreuther those comforts which he appreciated more than the society of the great and noble. Not that he in any sense excluded himself from that society. By special invitation of the Queen, he went to Windsor to have a long audience of Her Majesty, and expressed to Mr. Cusins his delight at the kindness with which he had been received. Altogether he liked to mix in the society of English people; and I remember more especially an interesting evening at Mr. Dannreuther's house, when he was the life and soul of a large and distinguished gathering, including, amongst others, George Eliot and Mr. G. H. Lewes. Madame Wagner, who speaks

English perfectly, served as interpreter, and her conversation with the great English novelist—who took a deep interest in music, although her appreciation of Wagner's music was of a very platonic kind — was both friendly and animated. "Your husband," remarked George Eliot, with that straightforwardness which was so conspicuous and so lovable in her character, "does not like Jews; my husband is a Jew." Needless to add that Wagner's aversion to the Hebrew race was of a purely theoretic kind, and did not extend to individuals—witness his warm friendship for Tausig, one of his staunchest adherents, and the earliest promoter of the Bayreuth idea.

The concerts at the Albert Hall took place on May 7, 9, 12, 14, 16, and 19, and were largely attended, although not largely enough to equal the vast sums spent in advertisements, salaries of vocalists and orchestral players, etc. To make up for the loss, two additional concerts at popular prices were given on May 28 and 29. Wagner conducted part of the performances on each occasion, and during the rest of the concert sat in the front row of the orchestra, following the music with obvious interest, and himself the observed of all observers. As a conductor he scarcely did himself justice on this occasion. To those who had seen him conduct the Ninth Symphony five years earlier, the difference seemed great indeed, and by no means accounted for by the lapse of time, although that no doubt told considerably at Wagner's age. The truth is that Wagner's strength did not lie in keeping great masses together by a firm beat, or in helping an orchestra over the difficulties of making acquaintance with new and intricate music. But when these difficulties were overcome, when the players knew their parts so thoroughly that mere time-beating became unnecessary, then a slight motion of the hand, a keen glance of the eye, would make them do things which a humdrum conductor could never think of. In London this perfect sympathy between the leader and the led was never established; there was not sufficient time for it, to say nothing of Wagner's ignorance of the English language, which made interpretation a weary and arduous task. Wagner in consequence made the orchestra nervous, and the musicians greatly preferred Hans Richter to him, showing that preference with a demonstrativeness which was probably not very agreeable to the most modest of men and greatest of conductors. In spite of all this, the artistic results of the Albert Hall Concerts were both striking and permanent. English audiences here heard Wagner's music played for the first time as that music should be played, and the impression received, and evinced by incessant outbursts of enthusiasm, was all the more remarkable because that music had to rely entirely upon its own merits apart from the powerful aid of stage surroundings. This point was strongly insisted upon by a writer in *The Examiner* newspaper, whose words may be quoted as the expression of contemporary feeling.

"On the present occasion," said *The Examiner* of May 12, 1877, "Wagner's works appeared before us under a new condition—unsurrounded, that is, by the pomp and circumstance of the stage, and depending for their effect on the intrinsic beauty of the music alone. That this should be done with the sanction and personal assistance of the composer has been the cause of some surprise and much discussion in this country. Wagner, it is well known, advocates the absolute blending of music with the dramatic action from which it takes its rise, and without which it loses much of its power and significance. In the abstract this is undoubtedly true, and the composer would have infinitely preferred to produce his works on the stage for which they are so eminently destined. Unfortunately this stage is wanting in London, for the present at least; and in order to bring before the English public an adequate rendering of his musical intentions, he had, not without reluctance, to accept the offer of a concert-room. But in this case also the 'ill wind' has not been without its proverbial good effect. It tends to destroy a prejudice, frequently insisted upon by Wagner's enemies, that, without the assistance of stage appliances, his music would be devoid of all intrinsic charm. The selection from the *Rhinegold* on Monday triumphantly proved the absurdity of such a notion. Here was no darkened theatre, no invisible orchestra, no elaborate machinery—merely a few ladies and gentlemen in ordinary evening dress, and in ordinary concert-room surroundings; and yet the rushing and gushing of the mighty river, enlivened by the gambols of the water-maidens, was placed before the imagination with a distinctness perhaps the more vivid as the ear alone conveyed the charm to the mind. And this effect was produced, not alone on the few devotees who might supply the scenery from their remembrances of Bayreuth, but on a vast miscellaneous audience totally indifferent, it may be presumed, to Wagner theories, and unacquainted with the mythological significance of Loge and Wotan. A similar impression resulted from the graphic rendering of the thunder-clap, when Donnar smites the rock with his hammer, and from the lovely melody which by its broad expansion suggests the rainbow bridge on which the gods ascend to their rocky castle. Our remarks are, of course, not intended to advocate the transference of Wagner's music from the stage to the concert-room, but we certainly are prepared to affirm that, without any external aid, this music ranks with the highest productions of the art, both as regards melodious beauty and perfect mastery of form. If the Wagner concerts were to serve no other purpose than to establish this fact beyond the power of captious criticism, their artistic result would be highly beneficial."

In a pecuniary sense the concerts were less successful. A very large sum had been promised to Wagner for his personal services in the matter, but when he heard that things were not going well, he declared himself willing to forego all remuneration with that generosity which if on occasion he expected from his friends, he was not loth to exercise himself. This sacrifice Messrs. Hodge & Essex, who behaved throughout in a straightforward and admirable manner, refused to accept, and a sum of £700 was eventually remitted to Bayreuth. But this Wagner did not expect when he left London, and the last words he uttered standing at the carriage window as the train steamed out of Victoria Station were: "All is lost, except honour."

The parting scene was an extremely impressive one. A small group of friends was assembled on the platform to bid the master God speed, all of whom he shook cordially by the hand, while those more intimate he kissed after the German fashion. From any other man this sign of affection would have been scarcely welcome, but the kiss of so great a master seemed to set as it were a seal on an important event in the history of art; and I remember well that the late Mr. Davison, whom I had encouraged to accompany me to the station, assuring him of the very best reception on Wagner's part, had tears in his eyes. The antagonism of former years was forgotten in this moment of general emotion and reconcilement.

When the news of the financial disaster got about, a number of men determined to wipe off the stain on the English artistic character, and a subscription was opened without Wagner's knowledge, and soon reached the sum of £561, which was duly sent to Wagner. But once again he gave an instance of that contempt for money which he invariably showed when he had any money to contemn. He had made arrangements that the royalties to come from performances of "The Ring" at Munich should be set aside to cover the debt of the Bayreuth Theatre, and the sum collected in England was accordingly returned to the subscribers, one of whom wrote in his surprise: "Strange things happen in the realm of music." A letter accompanying the remittance and addressed to Mr. Dannreuther deserves quotation on account of the noble spirit and genuine kindness of its tone. It may serve as the final and harmonious chord of the English episode in Wagner's life:

BAYREUTH, 22nd *August*, 1877.

DEAR FRIEND,
    When I found myself compelled to give up a considerable portion of the receipts originally promised to me for the concerts in London, so as to ensure the artistic success of those concerts, a number of my friends conceived the idea of covering this loss by a subscription, towards which you took the initiative by appealing to those interested in my art in England. Some little time since, and after you had issued your appeal, other and nearer ways to help me out of the difficulties arising from the deficit at Bayreuth have been found. I would therefore ask the favour of the honoured sub-

scribers, a list of whom you have lately communicated to me, to accept again the sums they have so kindly placed at my disposal; and I would beg of you to offer them all my warm and most sincere thanks for the sympathy they have so kindly shown towards me.

Most truly yours,
RICHARD WAGNER.

IV.

After having seen what Wagner did and suffered in England, it remains to inquire briefly what his music did and suffered there, what successes it achieved, what rebuffs it met with, and what its permanent influence on English art is likely to be. Perhaps it will be found that the questions here stated are in a kind of correlation, and throw mutual light upon each other; for it is a curious fact that Wagner's music, essentially and intensely dramatic as it is, has fared amongst us a great deal better in the concert-room than it has on the stage. When Wagner was over here for the last time and saw his work triumph at the Albert Hall, he witnessed, as I already stated, a performance of *Tannhäuser*, which he declared to be the worst he had ever seen. The Albert Hall Concerts were the germ from which the Richter Concerts sprang, for it was at the Albert Hall that the public were impressed with the singular force and delicacy and mental grasp which Hans Richter brought to the interpretation of Wagner's works, and which, by some hidden magic, he imparts to the orchestra, from the leader at the first violin desk to the last drummer. English audiences felt this very keenly, and they accordingly applauded Richter as they never applauded a conductor before; indeed, they hero-worshipped him as only prima-donnas, or fiddlers, or pianists are usually worshipped.

When Mr. Franke—an impresario who, unlike the majority of his race, was a musical enthusiast, and ended in the Bankruptcy Court accordingly—started the Richter Concerts, musical and fashionable London flocked to them, and his success would have been as permanent as it was brilliant had he not acted upon a very natural and logical train of reasoning. If these people—he may have said to himself—like Wagner's music apart from its stage surroundings, how will they not appreciate him when they see his work set forth with all the potency of action and of scenery? In consequence he started a German, or what was and for a number of years will remain synonymous, a Wagner Opera season at Drury Lane in 1882, and the result was disastrous, although not so disastrous as later on at Covent Garden, when the experiment was repeated, or as the pecuniary result of the Nibelungen performances under Neumann's management at Her Majesty's Theatre in the first-named year had been. In following the aforesaid train of thought, poor Mr. Franke overlooked two important facts. The one is that English people like serious music and like the stage, but they do not care for serious music on the stage. This is a confession which the present writer makes with peculiar reluctance, but which one can scarcely help making. Or else, how is one to account for such an appalling juxtaposition of facts as the following? Half-a-dozen or more theatres in London at which operettas of various kinds flourish, and which are of course carefully shunned by the musical public proper, and not a single theatre at which serious Opera in English has been performed for the last two years; Mr. Rosa, after having attempted that serious Opera in the metropolis for many years, abandoning such an attempt for the present, and worshipping at the shrine of Planquette and his congeners. How are the *Walküre*, or *Tristan*, or even the *Meistersinger*, to flourish in a city where *Dorothy* runs for a thousand consecutive nights? If before these lines are a year old they are reduced *ad absurdum*, if the mysterious Mansion House scheme for the foundation of a National Opera ever comes to anything, if the immediate or even the distant future brings us novel performances of Wagner's or any other good operas, no one will be more delighted than myself. But of all this there appears very little chance at present. It is true that the English performances of *Rienzi*, *The Dutchman*, *Tannhäuser*, and *Lohengrin*, were well attended, and that the last-named opera, during Mr. Harris's Italian season of

1888, drew larger houses than any other. But this can scarcely be cited as a triumph of the true Wagnerian spirit, for *Lohengrin* has received the *cachet* of general popularity; it is appreciated by numbers of people who have never heard or would not care for if they had heard, the master's later music-dramas, and none of these has so far been attempted either in English or in Italian on the London stage.

It remains a fact, then, and is indeed the second fact overlooked by Mr. Franke, that although the English lovers of Wagner's music are numerous enough to support the Richter Concerts, and to send a large contingent to Bayreuth every year, they are not numerous enough to make a Wagner season in our own midst a paying thing; and with this fact we have to reckon when we come to consider the second question above propounded—that having reference to the influence which Wagner's music has had, and is likely to have, on the English school.

A wider range of view here becomes necessary. It has often been said, and I have frequently said it myself, that Wagner has, for the present, ruined dramatic music in the same sense that Beethoven for a long period ruined symphonic music. Such colossi throw a shadow on the onward path of the art from which later-born and lesser-born men find it difficult to emerge. To ignore Wagner is, for a modern dramatic composer, tantamount to assigning his work to the dusty repositories of the past; to imitate him successfully is almost a matter of impossibility. Hence compromises have to be adopted, and a hybrid mixture of the old and the new is the result. Germany, being nearest to the cause, has suffered most from the effect, and unfortunate amateurs in that country have at present to choose between the insipid abomination of Nessler, and the dull and long-winded operas with mythical subjects and plenty of leit-motives which Goldmark and other serious-minded but not very powerful composers evolve from their Wagnerian consciousness. Hermann Goetz, the author of the *Taming of the Shrew,* who had something to say and said it in his own way, unfortunately died young, as did Bizet in France, where also the Wagnerian impulse has led to such incongruous results as one observes, for example, in Saint-Saëns's *Henry VIII.* Even in Italy a similar phenomenon is repeated. If Verdi were a younger man, and Boito a more industrious man, they might no doubt have worked out the problem in their own national fashion, and given us more works so instinct with genuine dramatic feeling, and yet so thoroughly Italian, as are *Mefistofele* and *Otello.* But whether Verdi will write another opera, or whether Boito will ever complete his *Nero,* is at least doubtful, and in the meantime competent mediocrity rules the day.

Considering all this, it is perhaps as well that the chief attention of our English composers is at present diverted from the dramatic channel; for in the oratorio also, and in the symphony, Wagner's influence, although by no means a *quantité négligeable*, is not of such immediate, such overpowering effect as it needs must be in opera. Here, also, the powerful impulse given by him has, so to speak, purified the air, has swallowed no end of formulas, has transfused the rigid mould of the classical form with the freedom of poetic spirit. Liszt felt this when he wrote and when he named the "Symphonic Poems"; Mr. Mackenzie when he conceived the beautiful dream scene in the "Rose of Sharon"; Mr. Hamish MacCunn when he took firm grip of his poetic and pictorial subject in his weird orchestral ballad of the "Dowie Dens o' Yarrow." That all these things would not have been written as they are written if Wagner had never existed, there can scarcely be a doubt. At the same time there is no sign of slavish imitation.

There is yet another respect in which the great master's spirit may be of infinite benefit to English music. The principle of *l'art pour l'art* has never found a more perfect earthly embodiment than it did in Wagner. He abhorred compromise as much as Nature is said to abhor a vacuum. His whole life was a continuous struggle for the high things in art as opposed to the lucrative pursuits of modern vulgarism and commercialism. He had an artist's love for the luxuries and amenities of life; but rather than write such things as set the modern fleshpots boiling, he would have starved. This he says plainly in the correspondence with Liszt so frequently cited in the course of these remarks, and, what is more, he meant it, and acted up to his meaning. Indeed, when he held forth against the Jews, he did not use that term for the Hebrew race so much as for the men—Christians, Jews, or Philistines—who had introduced the worship of the golden calf, the "smartness," and knowingness, and reckless striving for effect, into art. These things exist and thrive, unfortunately, in all countries of the old world and the new. The royalty ballads, which even composers of note and of talent do not disdain to pour forth, the oratorios and cantatas that have been written, with an obvious view to a rule over the country, as the phrase runs, are the specifically British emanations of modern commercialism. All these things are an abomination to the musician imbued with Wagner's spirit; and rather than condescend to them, he would break stones in the highways, or give lessons at young ladies' schools. There are, no doubt, such high-minded men amongst us; but can it be conscientiously said that the majority of English, or, for that matter, of Italian or German musicians are in this sense truly Wagnerian?

CHAPTER III.

LISZT IN ENGLAND.

EVERY ONE who witnessed the reception granted to Liszt on his visit to this country in 1886 must have been struck by the cordial—one might say, personal —form which that reception took. Such ovations had never been offered to an artist in England before —not, at least, since the days of Paganini. Quiet-looking and eminently respectable persons would stand on their seats and wave their umbrellas and hats and handkerchiefs in a frantic manner when Liszt entered St. James's Hall; and even before he entered that hall his arrival was announced by the shouts of the crowd outside, who acclaimed him as if it were a king returning to his kingdom, and not a mere musician, whom Lord Chesterfield and even Dr. Johnson would have generically and contemptuously described as "a fiddler." There is no doubt that much of this enthusiasm proceeded from genuine admiration of his music, mixed with a feeling that that music, for a number of years, had been shamefully neglected in this country, and that now, at last, the time had come to make amends to a great and famous man, fortunately still living. It is equally certain that a great many people who were carried away by the current of enthusiasm—including the very cabmen in the street who gave three cheers for the "Habby Liszt"—had never heard a note of his music, nor would have appreciated it much if they had. The spell to which they submitted was, as I said before, a purely personal one; it was the same fascination which Liszt exercised over almost every man and woman who came into contact with him or witnessed his public performances, which, fifty years ago, impelled the young ladies of Berlin to fight for a piece of horsehair from the cushion on which the virtuoso had sat at the piano, and which appertained to the more than septuagenarian, with his commanding presence, his noble brow, his flowing white hair, and the winning, albeit somewhat cynical smile, as much as to the beautiful youth of twenty-five.

The intelligent foreigner who, from these ovations and demonstrations, might have argued that England was the very centre and focus of a Liszt cult, would have been as signally wrong as that accomplished person frequently is. As a matter of fact, our admiration of his music is skin-deep. For a number of years not a note of Liszt's music would have been heard in London but for the devotion and self-sacrifice of his pupil, the late Walter Bache, whose annual concerts were carried on at a great pecuniary loss, and in spite of every discouragement from the majority of the press; Mr. Bache's sole purpose being that of gradually forming a circle of Liszt-worshippers, and of still more gradually expanding that circle from esoteric to exoteric dimensions. In that purpose, and especially in the latter part of it, Mr. Bache, it must be feared, has not been successful. Whether the English admirers of Liszt count by dozens or by scores is a question of comparatively little importance. That the multitude, even the musical multitude, know little and care less about the real essence of his music cannot be denied by any impartial observer. When any of the Hungarian Rhapsodies are performed at the Richter Concerts, or even at provincial festivals, audiences are generally carried away by the impetuous *verve*, the rhythmical piquancy, the brilliant national colouring of those marvellous compositions. The Pianoforte Concerto in E flat is, as a matter of course, in the *répertoire* of most modern pianists, and Mr. Hartvigson has more than once created quite a *furore* with the weird "Danse Macabre." But these things show Liszt the composer only in the two capacities of an interpreter of Hungarian, or, more strictly speaking, of gipsy music, and as a consummate writer for his own instrument, the pianoforte. Of the vast and new ideas by which Liszt's position in the history of music will be permanently made or marred, and which find expression in his "Symphonic Poems," and in his "Dante" and "Faust" Symphonies, there is little in these more popular efforts. And these symphonies and symphonic poems are no more, in a general sense, popular than Liszt's church music—his oratorio, "Christus," and his "Gran" Mass, neither of which has ever been heard in England, although the Leeds or Birmingham committee might do worse than place them in one of their festival programmes, were it only for the sake of the experiment. More than ordinary technical difficulties may partly account for this neglect, but such difficulties are no longer an impediment. Where there is a will there is nowadays a musical way, and if the English public really wanted Liszt, they would most assuredly have him.

The cause why no such desire exists may, of course, be explained differently according to different standpoints. Is it that English people, with their sound common sense, have seen through the vapidity and flimsiness of Liszt's pretensions to a high aim and an equally great power of execution in art? Is it that the same matter-of-fact way of looking at things prevents them from realising the subtle essence, the sublimated poetry of Liszt's imaginings? These are questions which it is almost impossible to decide definitely for the present. Here again, a wider view is taken than the subject immediately in hand would seem to warrant. Liszt's position in Germany and the rest of Europe is no more finally settled than it is in England; and the system which gives significance to his great orchestral works is still trembling in the balance, even of unprejudiced and liberal-minded judges. That system shows, no doubt, a certain elective affinity with Wagner's great reforms in the domain of the music-drama. It may have occurred to Liszt, although he has never said so in so many words, that even as Wagner broke through the old forms, and created a new form in the drama from the mere necessities of the poetic idea, so might that same poetic idea be turned to new creative account in purely instrumental music, the listener's fancy being expected to supply the events which actually pass before his eyes on the stage. The way in which he has gone to work has been explained at some length in the biographical article on Liszt, contributed to Grove's Dictionary by the present writer, and it may be well to repeat the gist of his remarks in this connection.

It is in Liszt's symphonic poems and symphonies, we are told, that his mastery over the orchestra as well as his claims to originality are chiefly shown. It is true that the idea of programme music, such as we find it illustrated here, had been anticipated by Berlioz. Another important feature, the leit-motive (*i.e.* a theme representative of a character or an idea, and therefore recurring whenever that character or that idea comes into prominent action), Liszt has adopted from Wagner. At the same time, these ideas appear in his music in a considerably modified form. Speaking, for instance, of programme music, it is at once apparent that the significance of that term is understood in a very different sense by Berlioz and by Liszt. Berlioz, like a true Frenchman, is thinking of a distinct story or dramatic situation, of which he takes care to inform the reader by means of a commentary. Liszt, on the contrary, emphasizes chiefly the pictorial and symbolic bearings of his theme, and in the first-named respect especially is perhaps unsurpassed by modern symphonists. Even where an event has become the motive of his symphonic poem, it is always from a single feature of a more or less musically realisable nature that he takes his suggestion, and from this he proceeds to the deeper significance of his subject, without much regard for the incidents of the story. It is for this reason that, for example, in his "Mazeppa" he has chosen Victor Hugo's somewhat pompous production as the groundwork of his music, in preference to Byron's more celebrated and more beautiful poem. Byron simply tells the story of Mazeppa's danger and rescue. In Victor Hugo, the Polish youth, tied to

> A Tartar of the Ukraine breed,
> Who looked as though the speed of thought
> Was in his limbs,

has become the representative of man, " lié vivant sur ta croupe fatale, Génie, ardent coursier." This symbolic meaning, far-fetched though it may appear in the poem, is of incalculable advantage to the musician. It gives æsthetic dignity to the wild, rattling triplets which imitate the horse's gallop, and imparts a higher significance to the triumphal march which closes this piece. For as Mazeppa became Hetmann of the Cossacks, even so is man gifted with genius destined for ultimate triumph :

> Chaque pas que tu fais semble creuser sa tombe.
> Enfin le temps arrive . . . . il court, il tombe,
> Et se relève roi.

A more elevated subject than the struggle and final victory of genius an artist cannot well desire, and no fault can be found with Liszt, provided always that the introduction of pictorial and poetic elements into music is thought to be permissible. Neither can the melodic means employed by him in rendering this subject be objected to. In the opening *allegro agitato* descriptive of Mazeppa's ride, strong accents and rapid rhythms naturally prevail; but together with this merely external matter, there occurs an impressive theme (first announced by the basses and trombones), evidently representative of the hero himself, and for that reason repeated again and again throughout the piece. The second section, *andante*, which brings welcome rest after the breathless hurry of the *allegro,* is in its turn relieved by a brilliant march with an original Cossack tune by way of trio, the abstract idea of triumphant genius being thus ingeniously identified with Mazeppa's success among "les tribus de l'Ukraine." From these remarks Liszt's method, applied with slight modification in all his symphonic poems, is sufficiently clear; but the difficult problem remains to be solved, How can these philosophic and pictorial ideas become the nucleus of a new musical form to supply the place of the old symphonic movement? Wagner asks the question whether it is not more noble and more liberating for music to adopt its form from the conception of the Orpheus or Prometheus motive, than from the dance or march? But he forgets that dance and march have a distinct and tangible relation to musical form, which neither Prometheus and Orpheus, nor indeed any other character or abstract idea, possess. The solution of this problem must be left to a future time. So much, however, may be said at present, that Liszt, as an individual musician, possessed to a marked degree that highest quality of the creative artist—genius. I use that weighty word advisedly, and with consideration of its much-abused meaning. Whether Liszt's compositions possess that absolute vitality and substance which are the only guarantees of permanent life, the future must decide; that they are the immediate and spontaneous expression of a distinct individuality is not open to doubt, any more than is the fact that they have given a mighty impulse to the progress of modern music in the direction of what we may call its poetic development. Absolute mastery of technical means, large-minded generosity, helpful love for the work of others, uncompromising expression of innermost feeling regardless of immediate popularity—these are the qualities which have given Liszt his place in history, and to which the musicians of this and other countries should look up as to a shining example.

But it is time that we should turn from æsthetic speculation to historic fact, from the consummate master whom we all saw and admired in 1886, to the little boy who came to these shores when this old century of ours was in its teens. When Liszt in the year last mentioned went to Windsor to play before the Queen, he remarked on entering the room to Mr. Cusins: "This is the place where I played before George IV. sixty and more years ago." He was alluding to the year 1824, when the great virtuoso for the first time trod English ground. Even at that early time he did not come as an unknown stranger to musical England; his fame had preceded him. He had already conquered a prominent place amongst contemporary virtuosi quite different from that of other wonderful infants, who at the time were almost as rampant as they are nowadays. In 1820, at the age of nine, he had made his first public appearance at Oedenburg in Hungary, with such success that several Hungarian magnates had guaranteed sufficient means to continue his studies for six years. For that purpose he had gone to Vienna, and taken lessons from Czerny on the pianoforte, and from Salieri and Randhartinger in composition. He had been introduced to Schubert and kissed by Beethoven, who after one of his concerts strode on to the platform and embraced the boy before the audience. He had then proceeded to Paris, where, although Cherubini refused to relax the rule excluding foreigners from the Conservatoire in his favour, he had become the darling of fashionable ladies, who petted and spoiled the *enfant prodige* almost with as much ardour as the British matron more recently lavished upon little Hofmann and little Hegner. His father, with a keen eye for the main chance, then determined to take him to England, at that time the Dorado of foreign virtuosi, where the golden guinea grew upon trees and might be had for the gathering. Neither was the astute Adam Liszt much mistaken in his calculations. "Master Liszt" was well received in fashionable circles; he played, as has already been said, before the King at Windsor, and if, as Fräulein Ramann, his faithful biographer, remarks, English etiquette prevented the ladies from smothering the boy with kisses, even as the French ladies had done, one can only regret that the rigour of that etiquette is so much relaxed in our more enlightened days.

His first public concert in London, according to the same authority, was given on June 21, 1824; and although society was to some extent drawn away by a "rout" at one of the Princes', and by the benefit of Madame Pasta, the hall was well filled, Clementi, Cramer, Ries, Neate, Kalkbrenner, Cipriani Potter, and other famous virtuosi being amongst the audience. The programme of this concert has not been preserved in its entirety, but it appears that amongst the boy's performances was an improvisation, a feat of readiness which in those days belonged to the virtuoso's most appreciated tricks. In *The Morning Post* of June 23, 1824, it may be read that the theme "on which Master Liszt could work" was supplied by Sir George Smart, who selected "Zitti, Zitti," from *Il Barbiere*, whereupon the boy began to "work" without a moment's hesitation, winding up with a tremendous fugue, or what the audience accepted as such. What impression these *tours de force* produced upon intelligent listeners cannot now be ascertained, for musical criticism in those days was in the stage of infancy, and little can be learnt from such contemporary records as: "The young Franz Liszt has exhibited his talents to many people of rank and to some of the most distinguished professors of the metropolis, who all agree in considering him as a performer that would be ranked very high were he arrived at full manhood, and therefore a most surprising instance of precocious talent at so early an age as twelve."

So much is certain, that Liszt's first visit to this

country was both pleasant and lucrative, and when the season was over the father and son did not return to Paris, but stopped in London till the beginning of 1825. During this time the boy completed an operetta, *Don Sancho*, which was produced on October 17, 1825, at the Paris Opera, the famous tenor Nourrit taking the principal rôle. Apart from this, young Liszt is said to have employed the leisure hours of his London seclusion—for he saw few people and did not appear in public during the winter—in studying English; but how much he acquired of that language and how much he retained I cannot say from personal knowledge, for he generally spoke French and sometimes German with the English people whom I saw in his society. Such, indeed, seems to have been his custom, for Miss Fay, the lively American pianist, remarks, in her charming book, " Music Study in Germany " : " Yesterday when I was there, he spoke to me in French all the time, and to the others in German —one of his funny whims, I suppose." After a flying visit to Paris in order to settle the arrangements for the performance of *Don Sancho*, Liszt returned to England in the spring of 1825, and in addition to playing in London made his first provincial tour in this country. His success seems to have been very great, and as a matter of curiosity it may be well to reproduce *in extenso* the first of his two Manchester Concerts:

Theatre-Royal, Manchester.

Thursday, June 16, 1825.

Messrs. WARD and ANDREWS

Have great pleasure in announcing that they have succeeded (at a great expense) in engaging

Master Liszt,

Now only 12 years old ;

Who is allowed by all those who have witnessed his astonishing Talents to be the greatest Performer of the present day on the

PIANO FORTE.

The Concert will commence with the highly celebrated
OVERTURE TO "DER FREISCHÜTZ,"
Composed by C. M. von Weber,
Which received the most decided marks of Approbation at Mr. Hughes' Concert on Monday Evening last.

Recitative and Song, "The Eagle o'er the Victor's Head" . *Rook.*
Mr. Roylance.

Duet, "Gay being born" . . . . *Dale.*
Messrs. Broadhurst and Isherwood.

Song, "Una voce poco fa" . . . . *Rossini.*
Miss Symonds.

Air with Grand Variations and Orchestral Accompaniments, composed by Czerny ("Reichstardt" Valse), will be performed by
MASTER LISZT,
On Erard's New Patent Grand Piano Forte of Seven Octaves.

Ballad, "My ain kind dearie, O!" . . . . . .
Mr. Broadhurst.

Round, "Yes, 'tis the Indian Drum" . . . . . *Bishop.*
Miss Symonds, and Messrs. Roylance, Bennett, and Isherwood.

Grand Concerto (A minor), with Orchestral Accompaniments, composed by Hummel, will be performed on
Erard's New Patent Grand Piano Forte
by
MASTER LISZT.

Part Second.

MASTER BANKS,
(*Only 9 years old*), *Pupil of Messrs. Ward and Andrews,*
Will have the honour of making his first appearance before the Manchester Public, and lead, ON THE VIOLIN, the favourite
OVERTURE TO "LODOISKA,"
Composed by KREUTZER.

SONG, "The Spring with smiling face" . . . . . *Shield.*
    MR. ISHERWOOD.

DUET, "When thy Bosom" . . . . . . *Braham.*
    MISS SYMONDS and MR. BROADHURST.

An Extempore Fantasia on the Grand Piano Forte by
MASTER LISZT,
Who will respectfully request a written THEMA from any Person present.

SONG, "A Compir" . . . . *Guglielmi.*
    MISS SYMONDS.
Violin Obligato, MR. CUDMORE.

SCOTCH BALLAD, "John Anderson, my Jo" . .
    MR. BROADHURST.

GLEE, "Mynheer Van Dunck" . . . . . . *Bishop.*
    MESSRS. BENNETT, ROYLANCE, and ISHERWOOD.

Leader . . . . MR. CUDMORE.
Principal Second Violin . . . . . MR. A. WARD.
MR. R. ANDREWS will preside at the GRAND PIANO FORTE.

The Orchestra will be completed on the following Grand Scale: 12 Violins, 4 Tenors, 6 Basses, 2 Flutes, 2 Oboes, 2 Clarionets, 4 Horns, 2 Trumpets, 2 Bassoons, 3 Trombones, and Drums; and to afford every possible advantage to the Voices and Instruments, the Orchestra will be so constructed that they will be satisfactorily heard in every part of the House.

Tickets may be had at all the Music Shops and principal Inns. MR. ELAND will attend at the Box Office on Monday and Tuesday preceding the Concert, and on Thursday, the Day of Performance, from 11 to 2 o'clock each day.

The Doors to be opened at Six o'clock, and the Concert to commence at Seven precisely.

Boxes, 5s.; Upper Boxes, 4s.; Pit, 3s.; Gallery, 2s.

The SECOND CONCERT will take place on MONDAY, the 20th inst.

At the second concert, given four days later at Manchester, we hear of a new Grand Overture composed by the celebrated Master Liszt, who will likewise perform an Extempore Fantasia, and respectfully request two written themes from any of the audience, upon which he will play his variations.

The change which has come over the spirit of modern music can scarcely be more strongly emphasized than by comparing one of these old-world programmes with what would now be done at a high-class concert. For this was evidently a high-class concert, at which a gigantic orchestra of forty players co-operated, not a mere ballad affair, which even in these enlightened days would show a medley of insipid components scarcely less incongruous. It is true also that little Hegner quite recently went through the farce of playing an improvisation on a theme supplied by one of the audience; but then the worship of that and other clever infants marked, in the opinion of all sensible persons, the lowest depth of musical cretinism. Sixty years ago this was different, and, as we have already seen, the first virtuosi of the age countenanced the marvellous doings of the little wonder, who, for a wonder, grew up to be a great man. What, by the way, one asks, has become of the new grand Overture, and what of Master Banks, pupil of Messrs. Ward and Andrews? Master Liszt, it should be added, was at the time in his fourteenth year, and not "now only twelve years old," as stated above. The ways of enterprising fathers and impresarii remain the same whatever changes the whirligig of time may bring with it.

At the conversazione given in Liszt's honour by his pupil, Walter Bache, at the Grosvenor Gallery in April, 1886, some of the old play-bills were exhibited. At these the veteran composer glanced with his usual complacent smile, which was increased to a hearty laugh when one of those present explained to him the curious mistake caused to his biographer by the peculiarities of our nomenclature. Like all clever boys, the excellent Miss Ramann gravely remarks, Liszt desired to be considered a man, and the pet names, "le petit Litz," "le petit Mozart," applied to him in Paris, were anything but welcome to him. How glad, then, must he have been to see his tender age ignored in England, and to be treated as a consummate master of his craft, as Master Liszt! Liszt's stay on this occasion was a short one, and need not detain us very long. He went through the usual round of sight-seeing, and was amongst other things deeply impressed with the charity children's singing at St. Paul's, even as Handel had been before him, and Berlioz was after him. He also went again to Windsor Castle to play to George IV., and the First Gentleman in Europe, who, whatever Thackeray may say of his shortcomings, was a genuine lover of music, was so delighted with the boy that he went to a concert at Drury Lane Theatre, and honoured the young performer with an encore.

Once more Liszt came to London in 1827, and, according to Miss Ramann, whose zeal is untiring in collecting facts and collating old newspapers, gathered new laurels. To this statement, however, a curious commentary is furnished by Moscheles, who in his diary remarks that this season young Liszt also appeared in London. He played repeatedly with his well-known virtuosity, which was even then highly developed, yet did not succeed in filling the small room in which he gave his concert of June 9. Of his Concerto in A minor performed there, we are told that it contained "chaotic beauties"; of his playing, that it surpassed everything yet heard in power and conquest of difficulties.

On his return journey the boy met with the first serious grief his life had yet known. His father, to whom he was deeply attached, died at Boulogne. This event made an overpowering impression on the affectionate boy; it marked at the same time a turning-point in his career. His widowed mother had to be provided for, and to that duty he immediately applied himself with the generosity and unselfishness peculiar to his nature. Together with his mother he settled in Paris for a number of years, and this stay in the French capital, at that time the centre and focus of intellectual and artistic life, became of paramount importance for his future development.

Hitherto his mental training had been comparatively neglected. Adam Liszt, his father, although an intelligent man in his way, had the ideas of the old school, according to which it was sufficient for a musician to write correctly on a stave of five lines, without troubling himself much about general culture. The boy's education, therefore, had been sadly lost sight of, and it was only his stay in Paris which developed the resources of his nature, and made him essentially a musician of the highest modern type, and a worthy companion of Berlioz, Wagner, and Schumann, all men of deep thought and wide knowledge. In Paris he was thrown together and more or less intimate with the leading artists and men of letters, with Victor Hugo, Lamartine, George Sand, Berlioz, and Heinrich Heine, who, in his " Salon," has drawn a curious and interesting likeness of the young virtuoso. The religious struggles through which his impressionable and mystically inclined nature had to pass belonged to the same decade. For a time he adhered to the doctrines of St. Simon, but the Abbé Lamennais led him back to the paths of Christian belief in its Roman Catholic form, to which he remained devoutly attached for the rest of his life. It is scarcely necessary to add that the mighty impulse of the July Revolution of 1830 found a responsive chord in the heart of the young musician. Upon Louis Philippe, the embodiment of the bourgeois and Philistine, he looked with unmixed abhorrence, and on one occasion rejected with marked rudeness the advances made to him by the Citizen King. At Paris, finally, in 1834, he was introduced to the Countess d'Agoult, better known by her literary pseudonym of Daniel Stern, with whom he formed the most intimate and permanent attachment of his life. By her he had three children, a boy who died in infancy, a daughter who married M. Ollivier, the statesman who went into the Franco-German War "with a light heart," and Cosima, the widow of Wagner, in whose arms he died.

The eight years, from 1839 to 1847, mark the acme of his career as a virtuoso. From St. Petersburg to Madrid, from Paris to Vienna, his artistic tours were as many triumphal progresses. Money, which he prized little, the friendship of Princes, and artists, and men of genius, and the love of women, which he prized much, poured in upon him in one uninterrupted current. These were the halcyon days of the virtuoso, when people asked only who played, not what he played; and amongst virtuosi Liszt was the unrivalled first. The lady amateurs of our day would stand aghast at reading in old newspapers of the demonstrations which their grandmothers indulged in.

II.

Liszt returned to this country in 1840, and this, his fourth visit, is the first which properly comes within the scope of this work, and must be treated at greater length accordingly. When he was here as a boy, his doings were of little artistic significance; he was no doubt a miracle of precocity, and as such deserved and received a certain amount of attention. But a boy, even if that boy be Mozart or Liszt, must of necessity be a more or less agreeable echo of the things he has heard and learnt; to speak of independent artistic conception in such circumstances would be a contradiction in terms. But when Liszt came to England in 1840, all this was changed; he had lived and loved, he had studied and thought, he had witnessed a revolution and sketched a Revolution Symphony; he was, in brief, in the prime of adolescent manhood, and a consummate artist to boot. To develop and garner his great gifts as a composer, his career had been too agitated; but as an executive artist he had created a type of his own, and it will be necessary briefly to define that type before the actual occurrences of his stay in England are passed in review.

Considerable difficulties are here encountered. The art of the executive musician, like that of the actor, is of vivid effect, but it has no permanence. How Garrick's Hamlet affected the unsophisticated Partridge, we know from "Tom Jones," but the means employed by the great actor even Fielding is unable to bring home to us. Liszt, it is true, has to some extent perpetuated his method in the numerous transcriptions and studies which he has published, to the number, it is said, of three hundred or thereabouts; but even these as they stand on the paper are notes only, that require his vivifying spirit in order to become enchanting realities. And where is such a spirit now to be found? Even Bülow, and Madame Menter, and Eugène d'Albert, only possess in a lower degree the realities which their great master and model united in himself; and Rubinstein, in the midst of his last London triumphs, was fain to confess that by the side of Liszt he was as nothing. Neither does contemporary newspaper criticism, in the way either of redundant praise or violent abuse, help us much. Perhaps comparison, odious as it generally is, may yield the most approximate results, although here also one should proceed with caution, taught by the misfortunes of others. The lady in Paris, for example, who thought that she had said something very witty when she exclaimed that "she would like Thalberg for a familiar friend, Chopin for a husband, and Liszt for a lover," was very wide of the mark. The elegant and formal Thalberg might perhaps have passed as a friend, and most ladies were in love with Liszt, and many of them no doubt would have liked him to reciprocate the feeling; but Chopin, the Ariel, the Keats of music, as a bread-winner, a protector, a father—perish the thought! We must look for our evidence to less witty and more competent judges.

The person to be compared with Liszt, is sufficiently

determined by the historic fitness of things. The only artist who was pitted against him by adverse contemporaries as his rival and equal was Thalberg, and that opinion Liszt, to some extent, countenanced himself. He was far above professional jealousy of the ordinary kind, and the two virtuosi, indeed, remained the best of friends throughout their lives; but when Thalberg came to Paris in 1836, and carried all before him, Liszt felt himself compelled to emerge from his Swiss retreat, and to remind French amateurs that he also was in existence, and also could play the piano. The two *soirées* he gave at the Salle Pleyel, and the Salle Érard, are matter of history, for they have been enshrined in Berlioz's glowing prose. At the end of the battle, if so it may be called, each party retained its own opinion, but in this all coincided, that Liszt had never before been heard as he had been heard when put on his mettle by the success of Thalberg.

As to the individuality and achievements of that artist, I am able to quote the testimony of so competent a witness as Mr. A. J. Hipkins, who has heard and befriended all the great pianists, from Liszt and Chopin, to Madame Schumann and M. de Pachmann:

> What can I say of Thalberg? A handsome, gentlemanly, chivalrous-looking man, in general appearance not a little resembling the late Prince Consort. He took his seat at the piano with an unobtrusive bearing that distinguished him as an aristocrat

among pianists, and he never disturbed that impression by any excess of gesture. He always used Erard's pianos in England, and was the best exponent of the qualities of those instruments. Like all the great *virtuosi* in the forties, he played his own pieces, which were a striking departure from the facile and graceful fantasias of Henri Herz, then so popular. His pieces were composed to show off his rare command of tone and the novelty of his passage-writing and treatment of the instrument. He adapted to the piano an artifice invented by the harpist, Parish Alvars, which consisted in playing a melody in detached notes in the centre of the instrument while rushing up and down the keyboard in scales and arpeggios as if there were two players and two instruments, the melody being made sustained by a judicious employment of the damper pedal. Although now so common as to have become stale, it was then an innovation that took the public by storm. Thalberg's well-balanced *diminuendos* and *crescendos*, the latter carried up to a sweeping *fortissimo* without in the least imperilling the quality of the tone, were achievements that no subsequent pianist can be said to have rivalled; and among his contemporaries, only Liszt, Henselt, and Leopold de Meyer could rank with him in quality of tone. It must be remembered that at that time the sonatas of Beethoven and the works of the other great classical composers were not appreciated by the average amateur, and Chopin and Schumann, who had written much for the piano, were as yet practically unknown. Still, great as Thalberg undoubtedly was, he lacked for me the poetry and charm of Chopin as a player, and the enthusiasm he excited must have been surpassed by the more startling achievements of Liszt on the one hand, and on the other by those supreme moments when Mendelssohn, as I have been told, gave full scope to his rare qualities as a performer. When Thalberg last appeared in London—I think about 1860—his execution was much impaired, probably through having discontinued the constant study indispensable to a public player. It is said, when he retired to his vineyards he never touched a piano again.

As to Liszt, innumerable competent witnesses might be cited, none of whom has spoken more to the point, and expressed the distinguishing feature of his style more tersely, than Wagner in his pamphlet on the Symphonic Poems, from which the following passage is extracted:

> He who had frequent opportunities, particularly in a friendly circle, of hearing Liszt play—for instance, Beethoven—must have understood that this was not mere reproduction, but real production. The actual point of division between these two things is not so easily determined as most people believe; but so much I have ascertained beyond a doubt, that, in order to reproduce Beethoven, one must be able to produce with him. It would be impossible to make this understood by those who have, in all their life, heard nothing but the ordinary performances and renderings by virtuosos of Beethoven's works. Into the worth and essence of such renderings I have, in the course of time, gained so sad an insight that I prefer not to offend anybody by expressing myself more clearly. I ask, on the other hand, all who have heard, for instance, Beethoven's Op. 106 or Op. 111 (the two great sonatas in B flat and C) played by Liszt in a friendly circle, what they previously knew of these creations, and what they learned of them on these occasions? If this was reproduction, then surely it was worth a great deal more than all the sonatas reproducing Beethoven which are " produced " by our pianoforte composers in imitation of those imperfectly comprehended works.

Wagner, it will be observed, speaks merely of one—the productive or creative—side of Liszt's genius. Of his feats as a virtuoso—his novel treatment of the instrument, which extends its boundary line almost to orchestral limits, his inspired readings of the great masters, his unequalled technique, his storms of passion, and his soft sighings—he has no occasion to speak. A description of all this may be found in the writings of Mr. Chorley, who, notably in *The Athenæum* of May 16, 1840, launches forth on a sea of epithets which shows how entirely his critical equilibrium was upset by the *afflatus* of Liszt's genius.

But perhaps it will be more to the point to quote the reminiscences which one of Liszt's most intelligent pupils has committed to paper. This is Miss Fay, a young American pianist who visited Germany in 1873, and has recorded her musical impressions of that country in a volume which amusingly combines glowing enthusiasm with a good deal of Yankee shrewdness. The portrait drawn by her of Liszt is singularly vivid and lifelike, as the following extracts will show:

In Liszt I can at last say that my ideal in *something* has been realised. He goes far beyond all that I expected. Anything so perfectly beautiful as he looks when he sits at the piano I never saw, and yet he is almost an old man now (1873). I enjoy him as I would an excellent work of art. His personal magnetism is immense, and I can scarcely bear it when he plays. He can make me cry all he chooses, and that is saying a great deal, because I've heard so much music, and *never* have been affected by it. Even Joachim, whom I think divine, never moved me. When Liszt plays anything pathetic, it sounds as if he had been through everything, and opens all one's wounds afresh. All that one has ever suffered comes before one again. Who was it that I heard say once, that years ago he saw Clara Schumann sitting in tears near the platform, during one of Liszt's performances? Liszt knows well the influence he has on people, for he always fixes his eyes on some one of us when he plays, and I believe he tries to wring our hearts. When he plays a passage, and goes pearling down the keyboard, he often looks over at me and smiles, to see whether I am appreciating it. But I doubt if he feels any particular emotion himself when he is piercing you through with his rendering. He is simply hearing every tone, knowing exactly what effect he wishes to produce, and how to do it. In fact, he is practically two persons in one—the listener and the performer. But what immense self-command that implies! No matter how fast he plays, you always feel that there is "plenty of time"—no need to be anxious. You might as well try to move one of the Pyramids as fluster *him*. Tausig possessed this repose in a technical way, and his touch was marvellous, but he never drew the tears to your eyes. He could not wind himself through all the subtle labyrinths of the heart as Liszt does.

Most people who have not heard Liszt, will probably think this kind of encomium gushing, if not childish; to those who heard him in his best days, it will appear only as a weak echo of what they felt themselves. The writer's personal experience will not, perhaps, be altogether inappropriate in this connection. I never heard Liszt in his prime, and upon the whole feel glad that I did not. When he was rushing through Europe in the manner of a meteor, some of the alloy which is apt to cling to such migratory bodies was mixed with the higher qualities of his nature; he was, in fact, a virtuoso, and a virtuoso of forty years ago, when audiences cared more for fireworks than for serious art, and although he was one of the first to alter that state of things, and played, for example, the later works of Beethoven long before any other pianist ventured to do so, yet he was to some extent influenced by the atmosphere in which he moved. But afterwards, when he had given up his public career as a player, Liszt liked to please himself, regardless of the ephemeral applause of miscellaneous audiences. Even Wagner, when he speaks of the Beethoven performances of his great friend, and calls them " creations in the true sense of the word," adds that one ought to hear Liszt play " in a friendly circle." It was in such favourable circumstances that I was privileged to listen to these revelations, and on no occasion with greater delight than on the last in the summer of 1884 at Bayreuth, where I had journeyed with a party of friends to hear the repetition of Wagner's *Parsifal*. Liszt never missed one of these performances, and was always surrounded by a bevy of princesses and duchesses, Russian, German, and French. At such times one did not care much to trouble the master with a visit, but being told by Hans Richter that he wished particularly to see me, I called on him at the house where he used to take up his quarters in order to avoid the crowds of visitors who always besieged Wagner's house, " Wahnfried." Liszt received me with the profusion of politeness, " gratitude for what I had done for his music in England," and the like, which belonged to his courtly manner, and always reminded one of his own saying, that if he had not been a musician he would have been the first diplomatist in Europe. He did not play at that time, and I did not expect to see him again ; but the next morning, at a little after seven, I heard a loud knock at my bedroom door, and when, with the disregard of the imperfections of attire which one acquires abroad, I asked the supposed waiter or chambermaid to enter, in came Liszt with many excuses for his early call. He always rose, he said, at four in the morning, and his time for visits was from six to eight a.m. Having shown the master into a more fitting apartment and finished my toilet in great haste, I had another long and interesting conversation, and as I accompanied him back across the fine old square in which that dirtiest and most malodorous of hostelries, the "Reichsadler," is situated, he asked me to come to his house that afternoon to hear some of his pupils perform. No sooner had the ladies of our party heard of this invitation than they insisted upon being included in it, and when this had been accomplished they demanded, with the urgency peculiar to their sex, that I should make the master play to them. This I knew by experience to be by no means an easy task, for Liszt never played when directly asked to do so, and on one occasion was said to have refused the Pope himself. Diplomacy, therefore, would be necessary, and this in the presence of the great *diplomate manqué!* We arrived, however, in due season, at the house of Liszt, whom we found surrounded with a number of pupils and by a miscellaneous company, including a nun and a Russian Princess, one of the most portly and amiable ladies I have ever met. The conversation turned upon general and subsequently upon musical topics, but what was in every one's mind—the wish that the master should play—no one dared to utter. At last despair brought me sudden inspiration. Happening to talk of Italian literature, in which Liszt, as in every other literature, was perfectly at home, I referred to the difficulty which the sonnet, with its rhythmical division into double quartet and final sestet, offered for musical setting, and added with perfect sincerity that the only composer who had completely overcome that difficulty was Liszt himself in his "Tre Sonnetti di Petrarca posti in musica per la voce." Citing the opening lines of the second of these sonnets:

> Benedetto sia 'l giorno, e 'l mese, e 'l anno,
> E la stagione, e 'l tempo, el' ora, e 'l punto,

I pretended to have forgotten for the moment the tune to which those lines are wedded. This was enough for Liszt. Bounding up from his corner of the sofa, he went to the piano and played the beautiful melody from beginning to end. This naturally led to the two other sonnets of the collection, and the ice once being broken, one piece followed the other in uninterrupted and delightful succession. Not being possessed of Miss Fay's youthful confidence, I shall not attempt any description of how Liszt played; I may, however, say the following. Our party consisted of a hard-worked and weary critic, a much-admired and therefore much-employed prima donna, a distinguished amateur, and one of our leading conductors, all case-hardened, one would say, against ordinary musical impressions. When Liszt had finished we did not feel inclined, like the young ladies of Berlin, to fight over fragments of his furniture; we did not even applaud; but when we left the house we felt that we had been in the presence of something supremely great, something unique of its kind, something, as one of the party expressed it, "as unlike any other man's playing, as Wagner's music is unlike any other man's music."

To return once more to the parallel between Thalberg and Liszt, we see on the one side smoothness, correctness, distinct rhythmical phrasing, in brief, all the qualities which one may sum up in the epithet gentlemanly or aristocratic; on the other creative, or at least re-creative genius of the highest order, powerful artistic impulse depending largely upon the mood of the moment and restrained by no regard for traditions or even for the written text; for it is too certain that Liszt, during his virtuoso period, played even Beethoven's E flat Concerto with such variations and embellishments as might occur to him at the moment. Between such extremes, English critics and English audiences had to decide, and in the paper war which soon broke out, the names of Liszt and Thalberg are continually used as the battle cries of the contending parties, although I believe the two never met in England. For although Thalberg was in England in January, 1840, he preferred not to wait for the advent of Liszt, and Moscheles says in his diary: "Thalberg is again in London, but is off to Paris, and will afterwards go to America. The competition with Liszt is probably unpleasant to him, and it seems that he intends to avoid London for the future." The great controversy is by this time completely settled, and to the minds of most musicians, settled in favour of Liszt. But justice requires us to remember that the greater man survived the lesser man by many years, that he formed a school of enthusiastic and highly gifted pupils, and added the fame of a composer to that of a virtuoso. *Les absents ont toujours tort* is a great truth in art as well as in life. But contemporaries of course could know nothing of this, and the nearness of the phenomena made true perspective an impossible thing.

III.

Liszt arrived for the fourth time in London on May 6, 1840, and his first public appearance took place two days afterwards. During the next twelve months he paid no less than four visits to this country, crossing the Channel backwards and forwards in meteor fashion, and extending his campaign to Scotland and Ireland. Apart from the contemporary sources I have consulted, Miss Ramann's account has been of much service. Here, as throughout her book, she has taken a most laudable care to arrive at the facts, and although in some instances she has fallen into excusable error, her narrative upon the whole is lucid and correct. Even more valuable has been the diary of Moscheles, who eagerly watched and sympathetically recorded the Liszt incident. The attitude of the famous pianist towards his younger rival is highly creditable to him. He belonged to an earlier school which was in danger of being thrown into the shadow by Liszt's titanic feats, and the artistic idiosyncrasies of the two men were as different as possible; yet the thought of jealousy seems to have been far from his mind. His utterances are instinct with genuine admiration, and although he did not and could not love Liszt as he loved Mendelssohn, he remained his friend to the last.

Liszt's position in this country was now a very different one from that which he had conquered twelve years before, when all parties were agreed in praising the precocious genius of the boy. His early fame was, indeed, scarcely beneficial to him, now that the fictitious charm of the infant phenomenon was lost, and that he had to stand upon his own unsupported merits. He represented by this time a distinct tendency in art, and that tendency was considerably at variance with the conservative instinct of musical England. We are too apt in this country to extend the rules of unassuming gentlemanly conduct to the domain of art, and to look upon the self-assertive attitude as almost as inseparable from the artistic innovator as charlatanism. "They wanted to make him out a humbug," a distinguished and intelligent member of Wagner's Philharmonic orchestra recently said to me in a plaintive tone. Liszt also they wanted to make out a humbug, and in a certain sense they were not altogether wrong. A slight ingredient of insincerity belongs almost of necessity to genius, when it is brought into personal contact with the public—a remark which by no means implies that every genius is a humbug, much less that every humbug is a genius.

The humbug theory was expounded with great vigour in *The Musical World*, while Mr. Chorley in *The Athenæum* praised Liszt's genius up to the skies. In those early days, before the daily press had acknowledged the professional musical critic, the weekly papers were the true mouthpieces of public opinion, and there is no doubt that both *The Athenæum* and *The Musical World* were influenced by and in their turn influenced large sections of English amateurs. In this respect their utterances are of historic significance. But apart from this it is amusing to see how musical doctors differed in the year of grace, 1840. "There is," says *The Musical World*, "a manner of beating his instrument (to pieces we every moment expected), that to our mind places Thalberg far before him;" and it is "unable to detect an atom of genuine feeling," and denounces "fantastic tricks with tune" and "elaborate caricature," against the player who "more frequently suggests the idea of a delirious posture-maker than a refined artist, and employs his acquirements on some of the ugliest and least artistic combinations of sound that ever found acceptance in a concert room." With regard to the same artist *The Athenæum* launches forth into the following tirade of critical enthusiasm :

> In the mere chapter of difficulty vanquished, language breaks down. All former most elaborate combinations of melody with accompaniment; all manifestations of independence, not merely of the two hands, but of the separate fingers; all difficulties of execution, whether as accomplishing the grasp of wide intervals, or the close, dazzling texture of semi-tonic sequences, principal or accidental, in single notes or triple chords; all former displays of rapidity—the lightning velocity in his case, never distinct from expression—have been already surpassed by him and not yet exhausted, since a treasury of countless new effects must be at the disposal of one so prodigiously gifted. Every variety of tone, too, of which his instrument is capable, the level diapason of the piano, the faintest whisper among its highest notes, and the deep bass sound of its lowest strings "is ruled as by a wizard." Here and there, too, as in the "Marche Hongroise," he draws out a sound rich, keen, and speaking, as distinct from its usual voice as the oboe is from the other wind-tones in the orchestra.

It would be as impossible as it would be tedious to enumerate all the concerts, private and public, at which Liszt appeared in 1840. With his usual unbounded generosity he assisted his fellow artists whenever they asked for his assistance, and his first public appearance, on May 8, took place at a concert of John Parry, the singer, in Hanover Square Rooms, when he played amongst other things his own Fantasias on the *Puritani* and *Lucia*, and his Hungarian March. Moscheles writes in his diary: " Benedict has him for his concert, and so have

Mrs. Anderson and Döhler, and those who have him not print his name in large red letters all the same, adding in the smallest of types, 'with whom an engagement is pending.'"

"A new fashion," Moscheles also says, "has sprung up since Liszt is in London. Concert-giving pianists print their own names in the programmes in black type of moderate size, and then add in red letters a yard long, 'the celebrated pianist Liszt.'"

Liszt gave two concerts of his own, at which he was assisted by no one—an unprecedented feat at that time, which, alas, has become too common nowadays. And he is stated in Grove's Dictionary to have invented the term Recital for the purpose. At the Philharmonic Society he played twice, and the programmes of both concerts are now before me. In those days the Philharmonic had not a conductor-in-chief, and the office during 1840 was held in turn by Cipriani Potter, Moscheles, Sir George Smart, and Mr., afterwards Sir Henry, Bishop. The fifth concert at which Liszt played took place on Monday, May 11, 1840, and was conducted by Bishop, and included, according to precedent, two Symphonies: Beethoven's "Pastoral," and Mozart's "No. 6." The general performance, according to *The Athenæum*, was the reverse of creditable, and Moscheles also speaks in a general way of the "soulless rattling through our German classics perpetrated by the orchestra"; Liszt, whose name, by the way, the Philharmonic printer had not yet mastered and persistently gave as Listz, played Weber's "Concertstück," which had been rendered in the previous month by Moscheles. Some of the directors objected to this apparent rivalry, but Moscheles over-ruled their scruples, pointing out that every artist had his own reading, and that it was interesting to compare two different conceptions with each other.

The enthusiasm seems to have been boundless, and in one instance at least took a very practical form which it would be difficult to credit if Liszt himself were not the witness. After the "Concertstück," musicians and amateurs thronged round the pianist, and perfect strangers out of the audience insisted upon shaking him by the hand. At this juncture an old gentleman in a state of great excitement came forward, and taking hold of Liszt's hand pressed a bank-note into it, exclaiming: "It was worth more!" Many years afterwards a friend in Miss Ramann's presence said to Liszt: "How very wanting in tact! Did not you refuse the money?" "By no means," replied he simply, "I thanked him cordially. I should have hurt the old gentleman's feelings if I had proudly refused his gift."

Miss Ramann, by the way, adorns the old gentleman with a "snow-white beard"; but that must be a mistake, for beards in those days were unknown in

London. She is also wrong in stating that Liszt at the same concert played his "Hungarian March," and carried the accompanying orchestra along with him "as in a whirlwind of fire"; that performance really took place at the seventh Philharmonic Concert, June 8; and the indication in the programme, "Solo Pianoforte, M. Liszt" (by this time the printer had mended his spelling), seems to exclude the idea of orchestral accompaniments. At the same concert Liszt played a Sonata Concertante for violin and pianoforte, by Beethoven, with Ole Bull; and later on three Études by Moscheles—"Most excellently and reproachlessly as regards technique," remarks that composer; "but his genius entirely re-modelled my pieces: they had become his Études rather than mine, yet they pleased me, and by him I should not like to hear them differently. His Paganini Études, which I heard on his Sunday *matinée*, also interested me uncommonly. His technique beats everything; he does what he likes and does it excellently well, and his hands thrown high into the air descend seldom, astonishingly seldom, on a wrong key."

The entry last quoted is supplemented by a few remarks of Madame Moscheles, which throw an interesting light on Liszt the man as distinguished from the pianist, as he struck the onlooker in the year 1840. "His high-flying notions," she writes, "are made most interesting by all the arts of dialectics. There is a good deal of satire in them, and that satire is like an ill-tuned chord in our conversation. The sugared charm of his most excellent French cannot make some of his principles palatable to me; they do not suit my German taste. However, we get on well together, and I like to listen to him without being converted to his views. We were with him in Hope's Picture Gallery, and had an opportunity of admiring his knowledge of the sister art. His own concert, Moscheles had unfortunately to attend alone because I had a cold, and you must be satisfied to take his delight from me at second-hand, just as I had it from his lips, for he is too busy to write himself. When Liszt shortly afterwards called on me, he brought me his portrait, his *hommages respectueux* written underneath, and for Moscheles a small box of cigars; but, best of all, he played to me the 'Erlkönig,' the 'Ave Maria,' and a charming Hungarian piece. He now intends to take a trip to Baden-Baden, and then to start on a three months' tour in the English Provinces with Cramer (at £500 per month), and afterwards, by way of relaxation, to make a journey to St. Petersburg."

Here we have a true picture of Liszt, from an intelligent source and not coloured by the extravagant admiration of the time. We see the interesting and fascinating youth quite at home in every branch of art, and with a Mephistophelian touch in his nature, albeit friendly and sympathetic with those he liked. That Liszt had what is called a tongue in his head, and that mediocrity and pretentious arrogance found in him a trenchant critic, is a fact of which his friends are well aware. Even his consummate diplomacy and his genuine kindness of heart were not always able to sugar the pill sufficiently; and together with the warmest friends that ever clung to man, he had as many enemies as such a progressive reformer and whale among musical minnows would by rights have. Some of his good sayings in London have been preserved, as for example, when after playing a duet with Cramer, he laughingly remarked: "J'ai joué un duo avec Cramer; j'étais le champignon empoisonné et j'avais à côté de moi mon antidote, le lait"—a witticism which the old master of Études capped by another scarcely less apt when he said: "De mon temps on jouait fort bien, aujourd'hui on joue bien fort!"

After a successful season, Liszt went by way of Brussels to the Rhine, where new triumphs were awaiting him, and returned to London early in August. Here he played, according to Miss Ramann, at several concerts, including two Philharmonic concerts, in September; which is an obvious mistake, for there are not, of course, and never were Philharmonic concerts in London in September. Neither was Liszt there in September, 1840, except for a day or two previous to starting for the Continent. He set out on his provincial tour by the middle of August, and finished his first week at Sidmouth on the

22nd of August. He played on the 1st of September at Bath, and gave two concerts at Cheltenham on the 4th and 5th of September, completing his first provincial tour on the 26th of September, and sailing for Hamburg three days afterwards. Here he gave six concerts, the receipts of the first of which, close upon £500, he transmitted to the Senate of Hamburg for the foundation of a pension fund for the orchestra; 10,000 francs out of his London receipts went to the Beethoven monument at Bonn; and at this time his liberality grew so extravagant that his mother and his friends became anxious, and persuaded him to engage a reliable man as his secretary and almoner. This was Belloni, who turned out a perfect treasure, who accompanied Liszt in all his journeys, and subsequently was very useful to Wagner in Paris, as is proved by the correspondence already cited.

Liszt returned to England towards the end of November, and was to play at Reading on one of the last days of that month, but did not turn up, having been delayed at Calais by storms. About the 9th of December he set out for Dublin, and played at the Dublin Philharmonic concerts (the same which probably caused Miss Ramann's mistake), and at Cork and Belfast. Scotland and the North of England followed in due course; Edinburgh, Glasgow, and Liverpool especially being mentioned; and Miss Ramann makes the astounding statement that he left the last-mentioned port for Ostend, and was overtaken by a frightful storm. While the other passengers, we are told, "returned to the inner recesses of the ship, he remained on deck with head erect and his long hair tossed by the wind, and listened to the wildness of unfettered nature." This highly impressive story, unfortunately, must be classed with the romantic French picture which shows good old Papa Haydn in a similar attitude, seated on deck and braving a great thunderstorm. Liszt, who was a very indifferent voyager, had, of course, too much sense to sail round England in order to get to Belgium. As a matter of fact, he left London by the Antwerp Steam Packet on the 4th of February, 1841, *en route* for Brussels, where, as a newspaper at the time remarks, with the holy indignation of italics, "he is engaged to perform at a concert on *Sunday* evening." Such a wicked purpose would have been properly punished by the aforesaid storm. But I fear the whole story is apocryphal.

The provincial tour had not been a success, and Lavenu, the impresario, lost money over it, whereat Liszt repaid every penny of the honorarium he had already received. "He told me so," said Moscheles, with a smile, "calling Lavenu a '*pauvre diable.*'" For he always looked upon money as dross, and he who realised greater sums than even Madame Patti, and might have built his soul a lordly pleasure-house worthy of Craig-y-nos itself, died comparatively poor. That he bore no rancour to the English people for their indifference is sufficiently proved by the donations of ten guineas to the Royal Society of Musicians, and to the Society of Female Musicians, now long extinct. But the indifference shown to him as an artist no doubt was more difficult to bear. He had, however, the satisfaction of playing before and being received with the utmost kindness by the Queen and Prince Albert at Windsor, a fact of which Her Majesty graciously reminded the veteran artist when she saw and heard him again forty-six years afterwards. The paraphrase which Liszt wrote of the National Anthem during his stay in England, may have been a kind of echo of the pleasant impression made upon him by the Queen.

With the sojourn in Paris which ensued and brought its usual triumphs, we have not here to deal. Liszt was back again in England early in May, and played the Overture to *Guillaume Tell* at Mr. Parry's Concert. We also hear of a performance given for the benefit of the Polish refugees by the Duchess of Sutherland at Stafford House, when an eye-witness tells us the assemblage was quite select, and limited to 400 people, and of two recitals, which seem to have been well attended. His power was somewhat impaired by a cab accident in which his left hand was injured, but so great was his energy and his contempt for physical difficulties, that the public scarcely noticed the difference. " In spite of the Horticultural Fête," writes Mr. Chorley in *The Athenæum*, "the attendance at M. Liszt's *matinée* on Saturday was numerous and distinguished. In spite of a weakness in the left hand, which with any one else would have amounted to disqualification, his performance left all other pianoforte performances far behind it, and so excited and enchanted his audience, that but one out of twenty, we are sure, was aware that he was playing with scarcely three-quarters of his usual power. A part of his programme calling for exertions beyond his reach was necessarily sacrificed, and supplied at a moment's warning by the singing of Mademoiselle Löwe and Herr Staudigl with a hearty zeal, for which both artists ought to 'count one' in the good graces of the public." At the Philharmonic he played only once, and it may perhaps be taken as a symptom of waning popularity that the directors availed themselves of his services, only to the extent of the pianoforte part in Hummel's "Septet." The horn on the same occasion was in the hands of Mr. Henry Jarrett, an excellent virtuoso, and afterwards so well known as the trusty and intelligent agent of Madame Nilsson, Madame Sarah Bernhardt, and other artists. Moscheles says that the public expected something tremendous, but that Liszt wisely refrained from titanic or extravagant things in this piece. "For," he adds, "the type of Liszt's genius consists in this, that he knows perfectly well where, before whom, and what he plays, and uses his all-powerful faculties as means towards the most varied ends." Mr. Chorley fully confirms this impression when he says:

> The classicists, again, must have had a convincing proof of the soundness of his attainments by his amazing performance of Hummel's Septuor at the Philharmonic Concert on Monday evening. This was played from memory—an effort prodigious enough, with any one else, to have absorbed all that animation, and force, and brilliancy which must belong to the moment's enthusiasm, or they become formal and fatiguing. Yet so far from this being the case, the artist was never more at his ease in the most whimsical drollery, thrown off at the spur of the moment, than when infusing a new vigour of life and character in Hummel's fine, solid composition; and enough cannot be said of his performance without praise trenching upon the boundaries of extravagance. The reception given to it by the audience will, we hope, open a way to our hearing other master works of the classical composers for the pianoforte, rendered with a like splendour by the same matchless interpreter.

Liszt's social relations with the aristocracy seem to have been here, as elsewhere, of a cordial kind, although he was in this respect slightly hampered by the arrival, very much against his will, of the Countess d'Agoult, who naturally was not looked upon with a favourable eye by English ladies. He seemed, however, to have been the constant guest at Lady Blessington's house in Kensington Gore, where such an appendage was no great obstacle; and Mrs. Grote, the friend of Mendelssohn and all musicians, received him with great distinction. The intercourse with Moscheles also was again of the most friendly kind, and we hear that on one occasion

Liszt made him a present of a most beautiful cane with gold top, beautifully chiselled; while on another occasion, when the two artists had been playing some four-hand variations, Moscheles wrote in his diary: "I felt as if we were riding together on Pegasus." Moscheles also recalls a pleasant link between the Hungarian master and English art when he says that at a concert given by Miss Adelaide Kemble, Liszt accompanied that gifted singer in the "Erlking" with truly overpowering effect. The acquaintance thus formed gave rise to a kind of epilogue to Liszt's English experiences, brief reference to which may well form the close of this part of the subject.

Liszt left London in July. He first went to Hamburg to take part in a great Musical Festival, and also paid a short visit to Copenhagen; but in September he was back again on the beautiful island of Nonnenwerth in the river Rhine, just at the foot of the Drachenfels, which he had made his home for some time. Here he met a party of English people who were journeying up the great river. The party consisted of Adelaide Kemble; her sister Fanny, the famous actress who had retired from the stage and married Mr. Butler; Mary Anne Thackeray; Chorley, the musical critic; and a few others. Adelaide Kemble had a touring engagement both for concerts and operas in various Rhenish cities, and Liszt, who highly appreciated her talent, co-operated with her on more than one occasion. Mrs. Butler, a prolific and ready writer, acted as chronicler of the party; and from her letters, written at the time to a friend, and subsequently collected in her "Record of a Later Life," some interesting information may be gleaned. On one occasion they witnessed an outburst of the enthusiasm, with which at that time the great virtuoso was regarded by his countrymen. Mrs. Butler writes:

> Our temporary fellowship with Liszt procured for us a delightful participation in a tribute of admiration from the citizen workmen of Coblentz, that was what the French call *saisissant*. We were sitting all in our hotel drawing-room together, the *maestro*, as usual, smoking his long pipe, when a sudden burst of music made us throw open the window and go out on the balcony, when Liszt was greeted by a magnificent chorus of nearly two hundred men's voices. They sang to perfection, each with his small sheet of music and his sheltered light in his hand; and the performance, which was the only one of the sort I ever heard, gave me a wonderful impression of the capacity of the only really musical nation in the world.

The lively lady's musical culture was scarcely such as to enable her to estimate Liszt's importance in the history of music; and when she says in an off-hand manner that "Liszt never composed any very good music," she is of course talking of what she does not understand. The following remarks as to Liszt the man and the musician will, however, be read with some interest, as the expression of an intelligent amateur who knew the master in his prime:

> Liszt was at this time a young man, in the very prime and perfection of his extraordinary talent, and at the height of his great celebrity. He was extremely handsome; his features were finely chiselled, and the expression of his face, especially when under the

inspiration of playing, strikingly grand and commanding. Of all the pianists that I have ever heard—and I have heard all the most celebrated of my time—he was undoubtedly the first for fire, power, and brilliancy of execution. His style, which was strictly original, and an innovation upon all that had preceded it, may be called the "Sturm und Drang," or seven-leagued-boot style of playing on the piano; and, in listening to him, it was difficult to believe that he had no more than the average number of fingers, or that they were of the average length—but that indeed they were not. He had stretched his hands like a pair of kid gloves, and accomplished the most incredible distances, while executing, in the interval between them, inconceivable musical feats with his three middle fingers. None of his musical contemporaries—Moscheles, Mendelssohn, Chopin, nor his more immediate rival, Thalberg—ever produced anything like the volcanic sort of musical effects which he did—perfect eruptions, earthquakes, tornadoes of sound, such as I never heard any piano utter but under his touch.

IV.

Forty-six years elapsed before Liszt returned to this country. In the meantime of course mighty changes had taken place in English musical taste, and Liszt's music had benefited by them. That music had been heard on many occasions and in many different surroundings. Mr. Walter Bache started his annual concerts in 1865, and at the very first, given at Collard's Rooms in conjunction with Mr. Gustave Garcia (July 4th), he played with Mr. Dannreuther, an arrangement for two pianofortes of "Les Préludes." In subsequent years an orchestra was engaged, and most of the Rhapsodies and Symphonic poems were introduced in succession; the indifference of the public, and heavy pecuniary losses being unable to damp the ardour of Liszt's most devoted pupil. To Dr. Wylde belongs the credit of having conducted the first performance of the greater part of "St. Elizabeth" in this country; that event took place in 1870, and the principal soloists were Madame Titiens and Herr Stockhausen, both of whom hated Liszt's music, but being true artists, sang it of course correctly. At Mr. Ganz's Concert of the 22nd of April, 1882, the "Dante" Symphony was heard for the first time, and Mr. Cusins introduced some fragments of "Christus" at a Philharmonic Concert. Mr. Manns, at the Crystal Palace, also paid due attention to the Hungarian master; but more than in any of these places, Liszt's compositions, and more especially the Rhapsodies, were appreciated at Richter Concerts, where these works continue to stand next only to Wagner and Beethoven in popular favour. This much had been done to prepare the advent of the composer in 1886, and there were no doubt a good many English people who looked forward to that advent with the eagerness and interest of intelligent admirers. At the same time that admiration was limited to a very narrow circle, and even Mr. Bache would scarcely have believed that Liszt could ever become popular in England in the sense that Handel, Mendelssohn, and even Spohr were and are popular. There are at the outside, perhaps, 7,000 or 8,000 people who ever go to a Richter Concert; and what is that amongst the population—and even the more or less musical population—of London? To the outside millions Liszt was a *nomen præterea nihil;* still that name was sufficiently known and sufficiently honoured to make a favourable reception among us a foregone conclusion. *The Times,* in a leading article of the 5th of April, remarked: "That the world-famed musician will be distinguished to the verge of surfeit by every demonstration of hero-worship, is a prophecy upon which one may safely venture even before the event."

The Times was right, although it could scarcely have foreseen the gigantic and even exaggerated proportions which that demonstration eventually took. From the same article, the very existence of which proves the importance assigned to the event by the conductor of the leading English newspaper, it may be well to quote a few remarks bearing upon the different conditions under which Liszt's last and last but one visits to this country were made.

What will probably interest him the most, is to watch the changes which have come over English life and English art since the year 1841, when the railway was in its teens, and the reign of Queen Victoria in its infancy, and when the thriving suburb where Liszt, somewhat to the discomfiture of his admirers, has taken up his abode, was a country village surrounded by lanes and green fields, and not as yet looked down upon by the Crystal Palace. The contrast in musical matters between then and now will be found even more startling. The year in question was one of the most brilliant in the history of Italian opera, and a few amateurs still speak with enthusiasm of the glorious combination of Lablache,

Tamburini, and Rubini, Persiani, Grisi, and Madame Viardot heard in Cimarosa's *Il Matrimonio Segreto*. In the same year Berlioz's Overture to *Benvenuto Cellini* was hissed at the second concert given by the Philharmonic Society, at that time the chief and almost the only representative of high-class orchestral music, just as the Sacred Harmonic Society at Exeter Hall was that of the oratorio. In our days Cimarosa exists only in archives and libraries, and to Berlioz a place among the greatest masters has been conceded. The recent collapse of Italian opera at Her Majesty's Theatre is too well remembered; Exeter Hall is closed to music, and the Sacred Harmonic Society is dead. The Philharmonic Society still exists, but its importance for the development of music has been greatly reduced by the foundation of new institutions giving their performances in new concert halls, which are not, it must be owned, an improvement upon their less capacious predecessors. On entering St. James's Hall, with its hideous architecture, Liszt will probably think with regret of the charming Hanover Square Rooms, the scene of many musical triumphs, now serving as the dining-room of a club. Even greater than the havoc which the past half century has wrought among institutions and localities, is the change it has effected in the kind of music to be heard in those localities. The style of concert formerly in vogue can scarcely be realised by the present generation of serious amateurs. It was governed by the virtuoso, to whose demands every other consideration had to yield. As long as a large number of famous names was in the programme, the kind of music performed was of comparatively little importance. The late Sir Julius Benedict's annual concerts may be cited as the last survival of a type fortunately now extinct. A pianist who appeared at this kind of entertainment would, after playing a show piece or two, "respectfully request two written themes from any of his audience, upon which he would play his variations." The words we have quoted are literally taken from the programme of a concert by Liszt, who was always famous for his improvisations. Nowadays we do not expect a musician, any more than a poet, to be inspired at a moment's notice, and at the suggestion of "any of the audience." We look, in fact, upon music as a serious thing—*ars vera res severa*—and that we and the world generally do so is in no small measure due to Liszt himself, who, against the advice of cautious friends, and speculative managers, would play such works as Beethoven's last Sonatas, which at that time were looked upon as little better than the effusions of an inspired maniac. It was four years after his last stay in England that Mr. John Ella, the veteran musician still amongst us at the age of eighty-four, started the "Musical Union," for the purpose of producing the best works of chamber music, ancient and modern, which in its turn became the precursor of the Popular Concerts. We may anticipate without presumption that, as a whole, Liszt will find musical matters vastly improved in this country. The musician is no longer looked upon as a social outcast—"a fiddler," as Lord Chesterfield contemptuously and comprehensively called him—and if the widow of a wealthy brewer were nowadays to marry a fashionable singing-master no one would feel the horror and astonishment expressed by Dr. Johnson and his friends when Mrs. Thrale became Madame Piozzi. Neither would any modern English gentleman boast of his ignorance of an effeminate art, and disdain to acknowledge the difference "'twixt tweedledum and tweedledee."

The immediate object of Liszt's visit was to witness a performance of his "St. Elizabeth" at St. James's Hall, by the Novello Oratorio Choir, conducted by Mr. A. C. Mackenzie. The composer arrived in England on Saturday afternoon, April 3rd, and was accompanied from Paris by Madame Munkacsy, the wife of the famous Hungarian painter, and other friends. The express train from Dover was for his convenience stopped at Penge Station, and there some of his admirers and countrymen had assembled to bid him welcome. Herr Ferdinand Rath, the founder and vice-chairman of the London Hungarian Association of Benevolence, addressed a few words in the French and Hungarian languages to him, and Liszt replied in what the newspapers call "appropriate terms." From

Penge the party drove to Westwood House, the residence of the late Mr. Henry Littleton, the head of the Novello firm, where the composer lived during his stay in London.

It cannot be denied that the presence of the great man was in many instances made use of by mediocrities who endeavoured to shine for a day in the reflected splendour of his fame. Liszt appeared at a good many places where he certainly should not have been seen, and listened to performances which were not worthy of his notice. His own excessive good nature sufficiently accounts for the fact; but Mr. Bache and other friends should have known better and kept the composer aloof from such surroundings, although the task was no doubt a difficult one. They should also have prevented Liszt from playing in public; for he was no longer what he had been, even two years before, when I heard and saw him at Bayreuth. His gait had lost its elasticity, his eyesight was considerably impaired, and even at the piano the impulse and fire of earlier years seemed to have vanished. He had in fact become an old man—old even for his years.

In spite of all, however, he went through the "amusements" and ovations provided for him in the most sturdy manner, and allowed himself to be lionised like the grand old lion he was. What he thought of it all it would have been difficult to say from the perpetual smile that played about his beautiful mouth, and which, if it had in it much that was kindly, had something also that was satirical. He ate the dinners with good appetite; he played when he was asked to do so, and listened to other people's playing with apparent attention and delight; and it was only during the performance of "St. Elizabeth" that some of the audience were almost touched to tears by seeing the veteran composer slumbering gently in his stall in the first row of the side seats in St. James's Hall. By this time Liszt's part of the work was over. At the rehearsal of his Oratorio on Monday, April 5, he was sufficiently wide awake. During the greater part of the time he sat in the front row of the stalls listening attentively to the music, and occasionally giving hints to Mr. Mackenzie and Madame Albani as to certain modifications of *tempo* and expression which he desired. On one occasion he wanted more energy than Madame Albani, with whose performance he was evidently delighted, had given to the music; and when it was pointed out to him that according to the score the passage was to be *con molto umiltà* (with much humility), Liszt remarked, with a gleam of his old humour lighting up his expressive features, "Oui, mais elle est terriblement humiliée"—as much as to say that Elizabeth, although a meek and lowly saint, is also a Hungarian Princess, quite capable on occasion of giving her enemies what is familiarly called "a piece of her mind."

Liszt's presence at this rehearsal was what may be

called his first public appearance in London, and here already he received all those extraordinary demonstrations of popular favour which have been mentioned at the beginning of this chapter, and which were repeated with progressive ardour as his imposing face and form became more and more familiar to the public. On the evening of the rehearsal, April 5, he went to Neumeyer Hall, to witness once more the practice of the choir apart from the orchestra, and here he played on the piano to the delight, of course, of all those present. On the next morning he went to the Royal Academy, where a Liszt scholarship for young composers and pianists had been founded, thanks mainly to the activity of Mr. Walter Bache, in spite of the fact that Sir George Macfarren, the then Principal, was known to detest his music. Here he had to listen to a long programme of music and a speech from the Principal, of which probably he did not understand a word, and, in return, once more sat down to the piano and played to the pupils.

In the evening of the same day the chief event of Liszt's visit took place; and so important is that event in our musical history, that a more comprehensive account of the work performed, and of the manner of performance, may not seem out of place in this connection. The following is the account which appeared in *The Times* on the day after the performance, and which is here quoted in full:

The performance last night of Liszt's Oratorio "St. Elizabeth" was an event not likely to be forgotten by those who witnessed it. St. James's Hall was crowded to the last seat by an audience representative both in a social and artistic sense, and including the Prince and Princess of Wales and other members of the Royal Family. The reception given to the master is perhaps unequalled in the annals of English music. On driving up to St. James's Hall he was recognised and loudly cheered by the crowd in the street, and as he entered the concert room the enthusiasm at once reached fever heat, one salvo of applause following upon another in rapid succession. The composer occupied a seat in one of the side rows of the stalls, but after the first part and again at the end of the performance, the audience insisted upon his ascending the platform to acknowledge the cheers intermingled with an occasional "eljen" which rose from every side. Needless to add that Mr. Mackenzie, the conductor, and Madame Albani, who represented the sainted heroine of the Oratorio, received the tribute of praise justly due to them. Another incident of the evening remains to be recorded. In the interval between the first and second parts the Prince of Wales went into the artists' room and soon returned to the hall with Liszt, to present him to the Princess and the other members of the Royal party, with whom the composer engaged in a long and animated conversation. Distinctions so fully deserved and so graciously offered are pleasant to witness and to remember. Their description in print is, however, necessarily monotonous, and we therefore turn from the impression produced by the composer of "St. Elizabeth" to that work itself.

The performance of last night was the third given in London. To Dr. Wylde belongs the credit of having first drawn attention to the work at a New Philharmonic concert in 1870, and he was followed by Mr. Walter Bache, who conducted a very satisfactory rendering in February, 1876. On both occasions, however, some portions were suppressed. Dr. Wylde gave only the first part, and Mr. Bache omitted one scene. To Mr. Mackenzie and his choir, therefore, is due the honour of having given the first uncurtailed version of so important a composition. If, with all due regard for the genius displayed in it, we cannot concede to "St. Elizabeth" a place by the side of the two or three masterpieces of its class, several causes may be assigned. For one thing, Liszt is not a dramatic composer, and the Oratorio or Cantata, although devoid of stage action, is at least as much a drama as it is an epic. Liszt himself is aware of the fact, or he would probably have written an opera; but his admirers, and the public generally, think because he was one of the warmest champions of Wagner, and is in his later works no doubt considerably influenced by the style of the greater master, that therefore, the strength of both must lie in the same direction. The reverse is the case, as could easily be proved by the present work. Most of its beauties are of a purely lyrical or of a descriptive kind, while, on the other hand, that backbone of the dramatic action—the dialogue—is sometimes tedious, and always wanting in that primary force of expression which in Wagner carries one along as in the current of a resistless tide. A second, and a more serious defect lies in the nature of the libretto, which is totally devoid of consistency and logical sequence. The beautiful legend of St. Elizabeth—the same maiden who appears in *Tannhäuser*—has been treated by Herr Otto Roquette in the facile and inconsequential manner characteristic of the minor poet. Six scenes or *tableaux* are loosely strung together, and each of them is in itself sketchy and incomplete, and, moreover, encumbered by several irrelevant characters who say a few words and after that disappear again. In the first scene Elizabeth is a child four years old, and her bridegroom a boy, and here we meet with a prosy Hungarian magnate who, at the end of the work, finds his counterpart in another official personage—this time no less distinguished a character than the great Emperor Frederick II., of the Hohenstaufen dynasty, who comes to assist at the funeral of the departed saint, and expresses his sentiments in a long and prosy speech. The natural question why Liszt, endowed with refined literary taste, and himself an excellent writer, should have selected such a libretto, may be answered in various ways. In the first instance, it is not easy in Germany, any more than in England, to find a good libretto, and, secondly, both poet and musician were to some extent fettered in the choice of their subject. "St. Elizabeth" is in a certain sense a *pièce d'occasion*. It was composed by the desire of the Grand Duke of Weimar for a festival held at Castle Wartburg in celebration of the eighth centenary of its foundation, although the actual first performances took place at Pesth in 1865. The castle, as many readers are aware, has been restored and decorated by a series of frescoes from the brush of Moritz Schwind, which, *entre nous soit dit*, one would rather be without, in spite of the exquisite draughtmanship displayed therein. The six pictures represent as many scenes from the life of the local saint, and these scenes, poet and musician have undertaken to re-illustrate in their own fashion, forgetful of the principles laid down by Lessing in his "Laocoon," which treats of the "limits of poetry and painting." The difficulties thus put in his way Liszt has combated in a manner which evinces not only consummate workmanship, but, what is infinitely more rare, original genius. By all the means at the disposal of the modern musician, he endeavours to impart life to the indefinite types supplied by the poet. The "leitmotive" identified with Elizabeth, is of the tenderest sweetness, and its Hungarian origin is subtly indicated by a snatch of melody belonging to the tonality of the Hungarian scale. The long-winded address of the magnate who hails from the same country, also introduces the interval of the "augmented second" more than once—an interval which, although strange to English ears, comes perfectly natural to any peasant girl of the *pushta*, or Hungarian steppe. Again, the Crusaders, who appear in the third scene, sing a chorus which is based on a sequence of the Gregorian chant, and if their song is uncouth, and resembles in its orchestral treatment the *bénédiction des poignards*, from Meyerbeer's *Huguenots*, one can only say that two men of genius have employed similar means in depicting similar phases of thought; for the same fanaticism which impelled the Western world to a sacred war against the Moslems in the Middle Ages also incited the massacre of St. Bartholomew. Among the most beautiful numbers of the score we must further count the melodious and simple "chorus of children" in the first scene, and its *pendant*, the quaint "chorus of the poor," founded upon an ancient Hungarian hymn tune which precedes the death of Elizabeth. After her husband has been slain in one of the crusades, that unhappy princess is driven from Castle Wartburg by the wicked Landgravine Sophia, whom Liszt has painted in the most repulsive colours. Her utterances are the reverse of melodious, and Miss Pauline Cramer, who sang the part with considerable vigour, had to battle with the twofold difficulty of hitting the most unexpected intervals and of making her voice heard against an almost incessant *forte* of the orchestra. In this part it seems to us that Liszt tries to atone by exaggerated violence of utterance for the want of genuine dramatic power. Full of graphic touches, on the other hand, is the rendering by orchestral means of the conflagration which consumes the castle when the sainted princess is driven from it by the usurper. We next come to the character of the heroine, which the composer has evidently drawn *con amore*. He conceives her as a Christian saint meek and lowly, but with all her meekness she remains a proud Hungarian princess. This idea was no doubt in the composer's mind when at the rehearsal he told Madame Albani that at a certain point Elizabeth, although humiliated, was humiliated with a difference—*terriblement humiliée*, as he expressed it. The great *prima donna* had taken the hint. Seldom has she shown equal dramatic fire, seldom has her beautiful voice expressed so much, and expressed it so harmoniously and so free from affectation as in this music, which, albeit entirely removed from the sphere of ordinary vocal display, offers prizes of a higher kind to the intelligent artist. The *scena* of the fifth *tableau*, with its noble climax to the words "O childhood's dream," will be remembered among Madame Albani's most perfect achievements. Mr. Santley as Landgrave Hermann had comparatively little to do, and did that little as well as the limits of his physical power would allow him. A hunting song assigned to him is very like other hunting songs, only more difficult; and, apart from this, his music is mostly of a declamatory character. We should except, however, the first duet with Elizabeth, which occurs in what may without hesitation be called by far the finest portion of the Oratorio. This is the "miracle of the roses," based upon a mediæval legend of great poetic charm although of somewhat doubtful morality. To it the second scene of the Oratorio is devoted. A famine has fallen upon the land, and Elizabeth's bounty is extended to all the poor and suffering. At last her husband, Landgrave Ludwig, thinks it necessary to draw a limit to her charity. When he meets her alone and carrying a basket, he asks what it contains, suspecting her errand. "Roses," she replies, blushing at her innocent falsehood. But when he insists and opens the basket, the wine and bread she was taking to a sufferer have been miraculously turned into flowers. Heaven itself has converted Elizabeth's falsehood into truth. "A wonder has the Lord performed," sings a chorus from above, and Ludwig and Elizabeth join their voices in praise of the Almighty. This "miracle of the roses" Liszt has surrounded with the halo of musical art. The exclamations "A wonder!" "A wonder!" rise to a climax of mystic devotion unsurpassed in modern music, and the final chorus—

> " Blessing from Heaven
> On thee shall light,
> Type of the roses,
> Pure angel bright"

—is fragrant as with the odour of roses. Only genius of the highest order could have conceived and sustained the beauty of this scene. We have little space left to speak of the general excellence of the performance. Mr. Mackenzie, the conductor, had had the benefit of Liszt's advice and active superintendence, and had availed himself of that advantage in the manner of a conscientious and able musician. The result was a performance in which it was difficult to say whether the chorus or the orchestra was deserving of higher praise. Both were simply perfect. Mr. Whitney, Mr. Vaughan Edwards, and Mr. F. King did excellent service in the remaining solo parts. All three are baritones. There is, curiously enough, no tenor in the score.

It should also be mentioned that Dr. Wylde, having been the first to produce "St. Elizabeth" in England, gave a performance of the same work at St. James's Hall, on Wednesday afternoon, April 7, when the chorus was that of the London Academy of Music; Miss M. Macintyre and Mr. Reakes taking the principal solo parts. Liszt unfortunately was unable to be present on this occasion, having, by special command, journeyed to Windsor to have an audience of the Queen, who received him with the greatest cordiality; and, after a long conversation, asked him if he would play. Liszt consented at once and gave at first an improvisation. The Queen then asked for something from " St. Elizabeth," when he played " The Miracle of the Roses." After this came one of the Hungarian Rhapsodies; and Chopin's " Nocturne No. 1, in B flat minor," closed the performance. The Queen was delighted, and expressed her delight in her own gracious manner. The evening of the next day was given up to the conversazione arranged by Mr. Walter Bache at the Grosvenor Gallery, where a number of distinguished musicians had been asked to meet the greatest musician of the age. Many notabilities were present, and even Herr Joachim attended to shake hands with his old friend and protector, without however taking any part in the musical proceedings, which included the beautiful " Angelus " for stringed instruments; the chorus of angels from the second part of Goethe's *Faust*, sung by students of the Royal Academy; pianoforte pieces played by Mr. Bache, and songs sung by Mr. Winch. Once more Liszt sat down at the piano and played what appeared to be an improvisation, taking for his theme the March from Schubert's " Divertissement à l'Hongroise." On Friday the 9th he witnessed a concert given by Herr Emil Bach; and after that, by special invitation of the Prince of Wales, went to a smoking-concert at Prince's Hall, where he listened to a very miscellaneous selection of music with his usual complaisance, expressing himself especially delighted with the pianoforte playing of M. de Pachmann. On Saturday afternoon a Liszt Concert was given in the composer's presence at the Crystal Palace, arranged by Mr. Manns, with the following programme: "Rakoczy March"; Symphonic Poem No. 3, "Les Préludes"; Ballade, "Die Lorelei" (Miss Liza Lehmann); "Concerto No. 1, in E flat" for pianoforte and orchestra (solo—Herr Bernard Stavenhagen, his first appearance); Symphonic poem, "Mazeppa"; songs—"Es muss ein Wunderbares sein," and "Angiolin dal biondo crin" (Miss Liza Lehmann); solos for pianoforte—"Liebestraum No. 1, A flat, Fantasie dramatique sur Les Huguenots" (Herr B. Stavenhagen); "Hungarian Rhapsody No. 4, in D minor and G major." Mr. Manns conducted, and everything passed off in admirable style, the huge audience being untiring in its demonstration of enthusiasm, and mobbing the composer in approved fashion as he walked through the crowd, leaning on the arm of Mr. Bache, and preceded by two ministering policemen. "It was a pleasant incident," a newspaper remarked at the time, "and speaks well for the catholicity of our taste that on Saturday, while Liszt was fêted, as no artist has ever been in this country at the Crystal Palace, scores of people had to be turned away at St. James's Hall, who wished to hear Madame Schumann play the "Carnaval." Still pleasanter would it have been to see the two great pianists in amicable converse together, or to watch Herr Joachim leading the violins in the "Angelus" at Mr. Bache's conversazione. Neither is it easy to see what kept these artists aloof from one another. Liszt, forty years ago, was amongst the few virtuosi bold enough to play Schumann's music, and that composer dedicated one of his most beautiful pianoforte pieces to his champion. Liszt's early friendship for Joachim during the Weimar episode is a matter of history. Later on the paths of these great artists led in different directions, but not as different as the fanatics of the Schumann school and the Liszt school are fain to imagine.

On Saturday evening he was present at a reception at the German *Athenæum* and played to the members.

Such a week as has been summed up in the above remarks might have worn out a young and strong man, eager for fame and social distinction and the delights thereof. On Liszt, who was the friend of popes and emperors, and had been surfeited with all manner of ovations from his tenth year, these things seemed neither to pall nor to have any effect in the sense of physical fatigue, and so much was he pleased with the unexpected sympathy of the British public, that he determined to brave the wear and tear of a London season for yet another week. Of that week it will be better to speak with brevity, for demonstrations of the kind already indicated, after all, resemble each other very closely, and although they may be pleasant enough to experience, are not equally interesting to read about. On Sunday morning he attended Mass at the Brompton Oratory, and in the evening dined with the Prince of Wales. Monday afternoon, the 12th, was devoted to a Hungarian reception at the house of Dr. Duka, and in the evening he went to the Popular Concert to hear Joachim lead a Beethoven Quartet. On Tuesday he lunched with Lady Burdett Coutts, and on Wednesday evening witnessed a performance of *Faust* at the Lyceum Theatre, supping afterwards with Mr. Irving at the "Beefsteak Club." On Thursday afternoon he was present at the pianoforte recital by Mr. Frederick Lamond, the young Scotch pianist, and on Friday evening he conferred the same distinction on another pupil, Herr Stavenhagen, who had accompanied him to England. On Saturday a repetition of "St. Elizabeth" took place at the Crystal Palace, and on the following Monday he appeared for the last time at a concert of the Countess Sadowska. On Tuesday, April 20, he left for Dover by the morning mail, and crossed over to Calais.

A little more than three months after this memorable event, the news reached England that Liszt had breathed his last at Bayreuth on Saturday night, July 31, 1886. That news was felt by many of us almost as a personal loss. If it had happened before his memorable visit to this country, all lovers of serious music would have deplored the death of a famous musician, who, in his person, represented a link between the past and the future; as it was, we regretted him as a friend whom we recently welcomed among us, and who at parting gave us hope of another and longer visit. From London Liszt had gone once more to Paris, where further ovations and another performance of "St. Elizabeth" were in store for him; thence he returned to Weimar to recruit his strength for the Wagner performances at Bayreuth, from which he was never absent. He went there early in June to witness the marriage of his granddaughter, and after a short trip to Luxemburg, he returned for the Festival Plays. Already ailing, he insisted upon being present at the performance of *Tristan;* that generous imprudence, and the fatigues of the preceding summer, no doubt hastened his end. To his friends, who had at London noted the change which the last few years had wrought, the news of that end came scarcely as a surprise. Neither was it much to be grieved at, except in a personal sense. Liszt had done his work and had reaped the fruit thereof. The gift of euthanasia, so much desired by the ancients, was, moreover, granted to him. He died surrounded by his family and his friends, and in a place which, although not the scene of his own triumphs, was identified with a phase of his nature even more noble and more exceptional than his own creative and executive efforts. Amongst those for whom he worked, there was none he loved more and none worthier of his love than Wagner. The fact has, as it were, been emphasized by the locality of his death, and is remembered by the pilgrims who, after having visited the secluded and inscriptionless tombstone in the garden of Wahnfried, wend their way to the Bayreuth Cemetery and lay a wreath on the tomb of Liszt.

v.

In an artistic sense, Liszt's parting visit to this country cannot be said to have left a deep or lasting trace. That visit itself did not lead to the production of a single new work, and during the two years which have elapsed not a note of Liszt's music has been sung by the Novello Oratorio Choir, or any other concert society in London. This fact, alone, would be sufficient to prove that the observant persons were quite right who derived the reception given to the veteran composer from a personal rather than from an artistic source. Whether at any future time England will listen to the gospel preached by Liszt; whether our rising composers will heart and soul participate in the crusade of free poetic impulse against the rigid forms of classicism, the future must show. In one sense, however, Liszt's visit was of a considerable and beneficent import: it showed that English people can on great occasions be enthusiastic, especially when they feel that a glaring injustice of long standing has to be redressed. Liszt's nature was too noble and generous for him to bear any grudge against England for the artistic rebuff he had met with in 1841, and for the indifference with which his compositions had been received here ever since. The list of his pupils, quite recently published by Herr August Göllerich, contains a very fair sprinkling of English names; and the worst thing that Liszt, in his confidential correspondence with Wagner, had to say against this country was that English Philistines were not a whit less objectionable than German Philistines. At the same time, these things must have left some bitterness in his mind, and that bitterness was finally swept away by a display of goodwill and personal affection which is unprecedented in the history of English music.

CHAPTER IV.

BERLIOZ IN ENGLAND.

Of the three great masters with whose memories the movement called, for want of a better name, "The Music of the Future" will be identified, two had comparatively little connection with England. They came to this country, just as a hundred virtuosi and composers came and come to this country, in order to propagate their music or to fill their pockets with the coin of the realm. Their artistic devolopment would have been exactly the same had they never approached these shores, or had they never read a line of English literature. For although Wagner duly appreciated Shakespeare and Walter Scott, and Liszt was a great admirer of Byron and carried a well-thumbed copy of "Childe Harold" with him on all his wanderings, even as did Napoleon a copy of "Werther,' it cannot be said that either of them derived any artistic stimulus from these great writers. But this is entirely different in the case of the French master who completes the triad of the Musical Future. If Berlioz had not known Shakespeare; if he had not married an English, or at least an Irish wife; if he had not spent much of his time in this country, he would certainly not have been Berlioz. Perhaps he would have been Auber, or Meyerbeer, or a mixture of both. His mental and sentimental affinities with English life and literature began, indeed, years before the white cliffs of the *perfide Albion* loomed on the sight of the seafarer; and with these antecedent affinities it will be necessary to deal in a more or less summary fashion before the immediate subject of this chapter, " Berlioz in England," can be approached or properly understood.

When Berlioz was a little boy at Côte-Saint-André, he used to shed bitter tears over the loves of Æneas and the Queen of Carthage; and his youthful enthusiasm was roused when the name of Napoleon was mentioned within his hearing. Virgil and Buonaparte, and, in a musical sense, Gluck, were the ideals of his infancy; to them a fourth, Shakespeare, was added when the young medical student came to Paris, and when his poetic feeling widened and deepened with the things which at that time moved the literary circles of the French capital to the core. He arrived in Paris in 1821 at the age of eighteen, with the best intention of studying medical science, and with his head full of music. At that time, and a little later, literary Anglomania was the order of the day amongst the rising French school. The young romanticists, impatient of the unities and of the classical apparatus of the preceding age, used Shakespeare as the Shibboleth and symbol of poetic freedom and naturalism, just as Goethe had used the same name for a similar purpose fifty years before. Berlioz, the protagonist of romanticism in music, chimed in with this general tendency of the time. It can scarcely be said that he "discovered" Shakespeare for himself; for he did not then know a word of English, and had to be satisfied with the wretched translations and transmogrifications of Ducis and Letourneur. His knowledge of English literature was and remained to the end almost as vague as was Victor Hugo's of English History when he wrote *Cromwell* and *L'Homme qui Rit*. How else could he, for example, have adopted the abominable acting perversion of the deaths of Romeo and Juliet for his symphonic masterpiece; or calmly placed the excellent Tom Moore amongst the great pathetic poets of the world; while of Shelley and of Keats, or indeed of Coleridge and Wordsworth, he never says a word? So difficult is it even for the most intelligent reader to observe the true proportions of greatness and of depths in a foreign literature. To Berlioz, Moore was, in a vague way, the great singer of passion, just as Shakespeare was the exponent of tragic force. Fortunately for the artist, although unfortunately for the man, he met with an interpreter of Shakespeare, who brought home the beauties of that poet to his heart and mind in a very personal sense indeed.

In 1827, an excellent English troupe opened a series of representations at the Odéon, undeterred by the fate of their predecessors, who five years earlier had been hissed off the stage of the Porte-Saint-Martin for patriotic reasons. On this occasion the English theatre was well supported by the public, and was worthy of such support. Some of our leading actors, Kean, Macready, and Charles Kemble, appeared in Shakespearean characters, and Liston's humour was brought home to the Parisians in spite of the differences of idiom. Abbott was the manager. Only in the female department the troupe seems to have been somewhat weak, and the leading actress was Harriet Smithson, an Irish girl of no particular note in England. Miss Smithson was at the time about twenty-seven; a little more or a little less, for her age is variously given. She "owned" to twenty-five at the time, but Mr. Dutton Cook, in *The Gentleman's Magazine*, states that she was born in 1800, which would give her two years more; while in the official document drawn up at her death, the year of her birth is given as 1801. She was born at Ennis, Co. Clare, Ireland, and her father, a theatrical manager, had educated her for the stage. She appeared at various times at Drury Lane, Birmingham, and Dublin, and her most important achievement seems to have been her Lady Anne to Kean's Richard III. Fanny Kemble (Mrs. Butler, the daughter of Charles Kemble) speaks of her and her Paris successes in a somewhat contemptuous fashion. "The success of the English theatre in Paris," she writes in "Record of a Girlhood," "was quite satisfactory; and all the most eminent members of the profession — Kean, young Macready, and my father — went over in turn to exhibit to the Parisian public Shakespeare the Barbarian illustrated by his barbarian fellow-countrymen. I do not remember hearing of any very eminent actress joining in that worthy enterprise; but Miss Smithson, a young lady with a figure and face of Hibernian beauty, whose superfluous native accent was no drawback to her merits in the esteem of her French audience, represented to them the heroines of the English tragic drama; the incidents of which, infinitely more startling than anything they were used to, invested their fair victim with an amazing power over her foreign critics, and she received from them, in consequence, a rather disproportionate share of admiration — due, perhaps, more to the astonishing circumstances in which she appeared before them, than to the excellence of her acting under them."

There may be a good deal of truth in this, but Macready speaks of her in a very different way, and it is scarcely credible that all Paris should have gone wild over a mere pretty girl. It appears that Miss Smithson was one of those Celtic natures who, indolent in the ordinary course of life, are capable of great *élan* when properly roused. She had adopted the theatrical profession more to please her father than from any personal liking for it; and when Charles Kemble, on his arrival in Paris, proposed that she should be Ophelia for want of a better, she was at first horror-struck. She had never essayed the part, and hitherto her lines had been cast in comedy and conversational drama, rather than in the high places of tragedy. It is said that she locked herself up in her room for some time, but that when she came forth she had an idea of her own as to how Ophelia ought to be played, and had not so far been played. Being of a timid disposition and afraid of the jealousy of her rivals, she restrained herself at the rehearsal, but at the performance she acted, especially in the mad scene, with such realistic truth as to astonish everybody in the house, and not the least those on the stage, who at the first moment supposed that the excitement of the occasion had really driven her mad. The English troupe continued its performances with unabated success at the Odéon and Théâtre Italien during the winter of 1827–28, Miss Smithson playing the Lady Anne, Cordelia, Portia, and Jane Shore to general admiration. But Ophelia always remained her principal success. Little did the poor girl know how dearly she would have to pay for that success, by lifelong misery.

Berlioz adopted the new Shakespeare Gospel with the peculiar zest of his nature; where Victor Hugo, Dumas, and others admired, he raved. This is what he says, in language which defies translation:

Shakespeare, en tombant sur moi à l'improviste, me foudroya ; son éclair, en m'ouvrant le ciel de l'art avec un fracas sublime, m'en illumina les plus lointaines profondeurs. Je reconnus la vraie grandeur, la vraie beauté, la vraie vérité dramatiques. Je vis . . . je compris . . . je sentis . . . que j'étais vivant et qu'il fallait me lever et marcher.

Needless to add that Berlioz had applauded with the rest. To him also the fair Ophelia had appeared as a vision of delight; he had wept with her and murmured sweets to the sweet, as he strewed imaginary flowers on her coffin. Yet those sweets had not, so far, taken a musical form, and his heart was not touched. Dreading that such might be the case, he made up his mind never to see her again; but when *Romeo and Juliet* was announced, September 15, 1827, the temptation was too strong for him; and although he had the *entrée* to the orchestra of the Odéon, he paid for a stall out of his slender purse so as to make quite sure of a seat. This evening sealed his fate. Once more he resolved not to see the charmer again, and actually kept that resolution for some time. But in all other respects he submitted resistlessly to the inroads of the tender passion. He might have said with Goethe's Clara:

> Meine Ruh' ist hin, mein Herz ist schwer,
> Ich finde sie nimmer und nimmermehr.

His appetite was gone, and so was his sleep; for whole nights he roamed through the outskirts of Paris and the neighbouring fields, followed on one occasion at least by Chopin and Liszt, who vainly tried to console their disconsolate friend. Alas, that even in these moments of grief he did not quite forget the pose or attitude which in his nature was so strangely mixed up with genuine feeling! For what is one to think if one finds all these raptures and sufferings, including even his pale face, his long unkempt locks, and his disordered beard, minutely described in an article written by his friend Ortigue, but inspired, if not actually dictated, by Berlioz himself in illustration of the "Fantastic" Symphony?

So far Berlioz's passion had drawn its nourishment entirely from itself, without any kind of encouragement from its object. He had never spoken to her, and the letters he addressed to her remained unanswered and were finally refused by the exemplary young person. She was probably frightened rather than pleased at the strange attitudes of her lover, who glared unutterable things at her in the street, at casual meetings, or from his place in the theatre. A Mr. Turner, Miss Smithson's agent, good-naturedly charged himself with a message from the young French composer, and delighted him by the information that Miss Smithson's remarks on the subject had been kind, whatever they might mean. At last Berlioz arrived at a great resolution; he determined on conquering the indifference of his idol by his art. Miss Smithson, previous to starting on a tour through Holland, was to play two acts of *Romeo and Juliet* at a benefit performance of Huet, an artist at the Opéra Comique; and Berlioz, who knew the conductor at that theatre, easily gained permission to include an overture—it is not stated which overture—in the programme. These inspired sounds were to bear a message of passion to "his Ophelia," as Berlioz had come to name Miss Smithson. The overture was duly played, but unfortunately the actress was, at the time, in her dressing-room getting ready for her own performance, and did not hear a note of it; so the musical message remained undelivered, even as the letters had been. At last Miss Smithson started for Holland; and Berlioz, who as he assures us, quite by accident, lived opposite to her in the Rue de Richelieu, No. 961, saw her get into her carriage, and felt that the better part of his soul was torn from him. Only the promise of the easy-going Turner that he would report progress somewhat comforted the lover. But that promise was probably forgotten as soon as made, as no ray of light broke into the despair of the young musician.

In writing of these things one knows hardly whether to be serious or not. With Berlioz, attitudinising and real feeling were so strangely mixed up together, that it is impossible to say where the one left off and the other began. If any ordinary acquaintance were to tell us that he loved a lady much older than himself when a boy in knickerbockers, that after half a century, and after innumerable storms of passion, he met that lady again, and feeling that she had in reality held his heart through it all, actually proposed marriage to the old lady, we should probably treat such a story with ridicule. Yet Berlioz did these things beyond the shadow of a doubt. In the case of Miss Smithson also, there must have been a residuum of true passion at the bottom of much froth of vanity and obstinacy. That passion was strong enough to make him marry her when she had lost her money and her artistic position, but it was not durable enough to ensure his faithfulness to his wife. When Ophelia had become his own, she appeared a very ordinary mortal indeed, and the result was such as might have easily been predicted.

While Miss Smithson was gathering laurels in Holland and England during the summer of 1829, reports reached Berlioz that her conduct was far from exemplary; that Ophelia's indifference to her youthful lover had not extended to other men. The effect of this rumour (which was based upon pure calumny) upon Berlioz was, according to his own account, most terrible. For two days he disappeared from Paris, wandering about fields and desert places, and sleeping in ditches when physical fatigue brought momentary unconsciousness. It was probably during these days that the idea of the "Symphonie Fantastique" first dawned upon his mind. Goethe used to say that it was only after the agonies of unhappy love were passed over that he could embody those agonies in verse, and the same remark applies in this case to

Berlioz. For when he began composing the "Fantastic" Symphony, his passion for Miss Smithson had already begun to abate; he had sought comfort elsewhere. Ophelia had been superseded by Ariel. Ariel in ordinary life was called Mdlle. Camille Moke—Belgian by the father's and German by the mother's side. She had been taught the piano by Herz, Moscheles, and Kalkbrenner, and was all the time living in Paris giving lessons on the pianoforte, and already enjoying a high reputation in limited circles. Ferdinand Hiller, who was also staying in the French capital, had been enraptured by the talent and the piquant beauty of her sweet eighteen, and having no ready way of access to her, he asked his friend Berlioz, who gave lessons on the guitar at the same boarding-school where Mdlle. Moke taught the piano, to transmit his vows to the charmer. A less trusty messenger was never selected. Smarting under the indifference of Miss Smithson, and resolved to punish a person he had never spoken to, he could think of no better means than that of falling in love with somebody else. This accordingly he did with the ardour peculiar to his nature; and his new flame being capable of appreciating his musical genius and altogether more susceptible to the tender passion than this phlegmatic Irish girl, seems to have responded readily enough, throwing over, without a pang of conscience, poor Hiller, who acquiesced in the new arrangement with the best possible grace and even supported the lovers in their various troubles. For their course did not run smooth altogether. Mdlle. Moke's mother did not look upon Berlioz as a desirable suitor; and it was only after he had gained the Prix de Rome, with a cantata written while the July revolution of 1830 was raging in the streets of Paris, that she reluctantly consented to an engagement.

Before leaving for Italy, where the conditions of the Prix de Rome obliged him to reside for several years, Berlioz arranged a grand performance of his "Fantastic" Symphony; and, as luck would have it, Miss Smithson was again in Paris, and had just met with a signal fiasco in a French play written for her in which she did not understand the cues of her fellow-actors, and was hissed in consequence—an event which Berlioz observed with some pity not altogether unmixed with satisfaction. One day he meets her in the street and she takes no notice of him, whereat he nearly loses his senses with rage, so that his Ariel, to whom he flies for comfort, anxiously asks him: "Whatever is the matter?" The first performance of the "Fantastic" Symphony duly took place on December 5, 1830; but Miss Smithson was not present, neither would she have winced under this scathing musical satire had she been; for she had absolutely no feeling for the art, and was not even able to sing the songs in the mad scene in *Ophelia*, preferring wisely to spout them in monotone; neither was the effect of the Symphony upon the public as "terrible" as Berlioz had anticipated. The Ball, the March to the Scaffold, and the Witches' Sabbath made some impression, but the Scène aux Champs attracted so little notice that the young composer determined to re-write it then and there. Berlioz himself, however, was quite satisfied with his success, the more so that it had been witnessed by her who understood and divined his soul; there must, indeed, have been a good deal of applause, for it is distinctly stated that, in consequence of the public approbation, Madame Moke was finally induced to abandon all opposition to the marriage.

It is well known that that marriage never came off. Immediately after the concert Berlioz was compelled to start for Rome, and his friend Hiller, whose curious position in this affair has already been indicated, warned him not to rely too much on Ariel's faithfulness during his absence. On his arrival in Rome, in March, 1831, his first inquiries were for certain letters which he expected from Paris, and which failed to come to hand even after three weeks had elapsed. Berlioz during those weeks indulged his Byronic humour to the full, being, according to his own account, by turns intolerably sulky and amusing with his tragic airs. Mendelssohn and his fellow-pupils, who nicknamed him *Père-la-Joie*, laid wagers for a breakfast as to whether he would carry out his threat of returning to Paris, and thus forfeiting the pension which obliged him not to enter French territory for a certain time. At last he took his place in the *diligence* for Florence, and Mendelssohn, having lost his wager, duly paid for an excellent breakfast, of which the love-sick youth and other friends partook.

The 1st of April was the significant date on which Berlioz started on his journey of vengeance and retribution. At Florence he stopped for some days, enjoying the scenery and reading *King Lear*, and it was here that his anxious suspicions became dead certainty. Ariel, according to her aërial nature, had flitted. Madame Moke, in a letter, calmly informed Berlioz that her daughter, sickened by his absurdities, had married M. Pleyel. Every reader of Berlioz's memoirs knows his description of how he buys a pair of pistols and disguises himself as a woman, how he pictures to himself the scene when, entering her room, he will kill his faithless sweetheart with one shot, and blow his brains out with the other; of his journey to Genoa, and of his attempt at suicide there by jumping from the ramparts into the Mediterranean Sea. Considering how much Berlioz was, in blunt Shakespearean phrase, given to lying on occasion, few readers will be inclined to accept this absurd story in a literal sense. The truth seems to be that he accidentally fell into the water at Genoa and was fished up by some passers-by, and that the dose of salt water he swallowed brought him to his senses, although even for this story there is only Berlioz's own somewhat suspicious evidence. For in a repentant letter addressed by him to Horace Vernet, the Director of the French Academy at Rome, he distinctly says that he does not know who saw him fall into the water or pulled him out again, thus making inquiries impossible.

So much is certain—that Mdlle. Moke had had a narrow and lucky escape of becoming the wife of one of the most unmanageable men in the world. Poor Miss Smithson was to find this out to her cost before long; for Berlioz, after having embodied his experience or his confabulations in a novelette— afterwards republished in the "Soirées de l'Orchestre" —re-transferred his affection from Ariel to Ophelia without the slightest difficulty. On his return to Paris in December, 1832, thinking, according to his biographers, little of Miss Smithson or of Madame Pleyel, he happened to call at the hotel where the former lady had previously resided, and was told by an old servant that the English actress was then in Paris, and living in the neighbourhood. The news seems to have produced little impression on his mind, bent upon giving a large concert, at which the "Symphonie Fantastique," considerably rewritten in Italy, was to be introduced to the Paris public. Miss Smithson's affairs had in the meantime undergone a sad change for the worse. Relying upon the enthusiasm she had excited several years before, she had started a theatre of her own, and the public, having got tired of her, refused to attend; the result being heavy debts and liabilities which she was unable to meet. But Miss Smithson, though no longer a successful actress, was in another sense an object of interest to scandal-loving Parisians. Every one except herself knew that the "Fantastic" Symphony had been inspired by her, and it was upon this fact that Berlioz's friends formed a scheme in which one sincerely hopes that the composer, well versed though he was in all the arts of *réclame,* did not participate. M. Schlesinger, the publisher, offered her a box for Berlioz's concert, and on entering the theatre she was surprised to observe that all eyes were turned towards her. The Symphony on this occasion was followed by the melologue "Lélio," in which, as every one knows, the desperate musician returns to life and to his art. This "Lélio" is in reality a collection of miscellaneous pieces written at various times, and slightly connected by a thread of prose, its chief component being the Fantasia on Shakespeare's *Tempest* written in celebration of Ariel. Of this circumstance, of course, Miss Smithson was totally unaware; but on the other hand the explanatory programme of the Symphony seems to have struck her as somewhat analogous to Berlioz's case; and when in the *entr'acte* Schlesinger went to her box and gave her to understand that the music was all about herself, the good-natured girl shed some tears of sympathy, observed and keenly relished by Berlioz, who sat in the orchestra gazing at her all the while.

These idle tears sealed her fate. She permitted Berlioz to call upon her, and he proposed marriage almost at once. The lady was not unwilling to listen to him, but the two families strongly objected, and the consent of the old medical man at Côte-Saint-André had finally to be obtained by the legal form known in France as *Sommations respectueuses*. The engagement was not without stormy episodes, and for a short time was actually broken off. On one occasion Berlioz, according to his own statement, carried out the programme of his own Symphony, and took poison in Miss Smithson's presence, but was induced by her despair to save his life by means of an emetic. Berlioz could not get over the calumnies which had been uttered against his betrothed, and it was not till after marriage that he acknowledged their absolute futility. On the other hand a good friend had written to Miss Smithson from London that her lover was subject to epileptic fits. Unpleasantnesses of this kind much disturbed their mutual relations, and might have led to a permanent breach but for an accident which happened to Miss Smithson, when, descending from her carriage, she fell and broke her leg. It is in the highest degree to Berlioz's credit that now, when his betrothed was both ill and ruined, he insisted upon the speedy celebration of the marriage, which accordingly took place on October 3, 1833, at the English Embassy; Liszt and a few friends being present.

The honeymoon was spent at Vincennes, and there, and later on at their rooms in the Montmartre Quarter, the young couple seem to have passed several happy months. Eugène Sue, Legouvé, Liszt, and others, frequently dropped in of an evening to chat and make music over a cup of English tea. A letter addressed at this time by Berlioz to his intimate friend Ferrand, describes these halcyon days in this sentimental manner: "Harriet is a delicious being, she is Ophelia all over, not Juliet; for that she has not sufficient passionate emotion; she is tender, soft, and timid. Sometimes, when we are alone and silent, she, leaning on my shoulder with her hand on my forehead, or in one of those graceful poses never dreamt of by painter, I see her weeping between smiles. 'What is it, poor sweetheart?' 'Nothing; my heart is so full. I am thinking how dearly you have bought me, how you have suffered for me; let me weep or I lose my breath.' And I listen while she weeps quietly, until she says to me: 'Sing, Hector, sing.' Then I began the 'Scène du bal' which she loves so much; the 'Scène aux Champs' makes her so sad that she will not listen to it. She is a *sensitive* nature; in truth I never imagined that she was so impressionable; but she has no musical education, and, would you believe it, she likes to hear certain trivialities of Auber! She does not think them *beautiful,* but *pretty.*"

One likes to linger over these few days of happiness, and to remember that Berlioz, at the beginning of his marriage, behaved extremely well to his bride. By her imprudent theatrical speculation she had involved herself in heavy debts, and these her husband, out of his small pittance, paid off with the most laudable honesty, working like a slave to meet the expenses of the household, soon increased by the birth of a child, fortunately the only issue of the marriage. At first Madame Berlioz thought of continuing her theatrical career, and actually appeared in the fourth act of *Hamlet* at a grand miscellaneous performance arranged by her husband. But the [public received her coldly, while another actress carried off the laurels of the evening, and after this rebuff the matter was given up as hopeless, although another spasmodic attempt is recorded in 1837. In the meantime, a sad change had come over the household in the Rue-Saint-Denis. Madame Berlioz continued to weep, but she no longer leant on her husband's shoulder, neither did she ask him to sing any more. Terrible disharmonies had taken the place of melody divine. Who is to say which side was most responsible for the quarrels which became the order of the day, and which even the presence of the child could not restrain? It has been asserted that Madame Berlioz was partial to her native whisky, although this charge has been vigorously denied in other quarters. What is more certain is that there was no deep sympathy between the pair. Madame Berlioz had no more education than actresses usually have, and her musical knowledge was *nil;* worst of all, she admired Auber, as we have already seen. This was an unpardonable sin. M. Legouvé, one of Berlioz's earliest and most attached friends, has put the matter very fairly. He says that the parts of the two lovers were entirely reversed after marriage. At first Miss Smithson cared little for her eccentric admirer, but when she came to know him and to submit to the charm of his nature, she became violently attached to him, in the same measure as his own passion for the Ophelia of his dreams, whom time and close intercourse had changed into an elderly woman, who looked older than she was, and was older than her husband, grew cooler and cooler. Terrible scenes of jealousy ensued. Berlioz moved amongst the profession which, whatever its advocates may say, and whatever shining exceptions may be cited, is not the best school of the domestic virtues; and the temptations placed in his way would have turned a stronger head than that of Berlioz. His wife, no doubt, had rivals, and she discovered rivals where there were none. She ransacked drawers and coat-pockets for amorous missives; and every favourable notice of a lady in one of Berlioz's *feuilletons* in the *Journal des Débats* was a piece of evidence. All this, of course, was trying enough, but Berlioz having worried his wife into marriage against her will, had exceptional obligations towards her. What one likes least in his conduct is that he tries to whitewash himself. His wife's temper and jealousy, he says, "were intolerable, and they were without cause." That there was only too much cause was sufficiently proved when Berlioz left his house, quietly taking leave of his wife in a letter, and started for Brussels in the company of Mdlle. Martin Recio, a singer, and, as Nemesis would have it, an atrociously bad singer, who sometimes brought Berlioz to the verge of despair by insisting upon singing at his concerts. Hiller tells an amusing story of Berlioz taking French leave of his *inamorata* and journeying from Frankfort to Weimar, only to find there, in a few days, the irrepressible Mdlle. Recio, who joined him after having discovered his destination at the *diligence* office.

Berlioz never returned to his wife; but he provided for her as liberally as his limited means would allow, and occasionally visited her in a friendly way. During her last illness he took the most tender care of her, and it would be quite a mistake to think that the grief he expressed at her death (March 3, 1854) was not genuine. The letter written to his son on that occasion is one of the most pathetic things one can read. "You will never know," he says, "what your mother and myself have suffered through one another, and these sufferings were a link between us. I found it as impossible to live with her as to leave her." Seven months afterwards Mdlle. Recio became Madame Berlioz number two.

One good result may be traced to the ill-fated union of the French composer with the English actress. Miss Smithson appeared to him and won his heart in the character of a kind of Shakespearean muse; she embodied to him all the thoughts and passions to which the greatest poet in the world had given expression, and there is no doubt that, in his mind, love of Shakespeare and love of Miss Smithson were convertible terms. His interest in our literature generally, was kept alive by similar means. Whether the pair, even in their honeymoon, read English together, whether Miss Smithson informed her husband, as even she might have informed him, that the agreeable Tom Moore was not a luminary of Shakespearean magnitude, there is no means of knowing. Certain it is, that ever after the performances of the English troupe in Paris, the French composer took a warm and active interest in English poetry and fiction. Although incapable of judging literary merit to a nicety, he was of course fully alive to imaginative beauties; and those beauties found a reflex in his music. His acknowledged masterpiece is founded upon *Romeo and Juliet*, strangely cut about and transmogrified after the fashion of Berlioz, but still essentially retaining the spirit of Shakespeare and worthy of that spirit. The overtures to *Waverley* and to *Rob Roy*, the latter no longer in existence, speak of the influence of Walter Scott. The overture to *King Lear*; a ballad, "La Mort d'Ophélie," dated London, July, 1884; the Funeral March for the last scene of *Hamlet*, written in the same year, and now forming No. 3 of *Tristia*, Op. 18. The opera, *Béatrice et Bénédict*, and the "Tempest" Fantasia inserted in *Lélio*, are further Shakespearean reminiscences. The "neuf melodies Irlandaises" dedicated to Moore, and as unlike Irish melodies as can possibly be imagined, belong to the same phase of thought, as does also the opera, *La Nonne Sanglante*, founded upon Lewis's sensational "Monk." At this opera, to a libretto by Scribe, Berlioz worked very hard, although he destroyed what he had written, when the directors of the Grand Opera withdrew their offer of putting it on the stage, with the connivance, it appears, of Scribe himself. The book was offered to Verdi and Halévy, but both of them refused to deal with it out of regard for Berlioz, who, they considered, had been very shabbily treated in the matter. Finally Gounod accepted the libretto, and his opera was performed in 1854, and met with a complete *fiasco*. The overture "The Corsair," and, it must be presumed, "Harold in Italy," treat of Byronian subjects. It may be mentioned in parenthesis that in his choice of subjects the French Beethoven, as his countrymen have come to call him, was singularly unpatriotic. Goethe's *Faust*, the autobiography of Benvenuto Cellini, Virgil's *Æneid*, in addition to English works—these were the sources from which he loved to draw inspiration. Not a single one of his important works is taken from French literature or French history; for that the "Requiem" was composed for one patriotic occasion and performed on another, counts little in the matter. Perhaps these foreign sympathies of the composer had something to do with the neglect of his countymen, under which he writhed all his life although he pretended to despise it.

II.

I have taken some trouble, and occupied perhaps more space than the reader may think necessary, in tracing the links of the chain which connected Berlioz the artist with English literature long before the man set foot on English soil. In these devious ways M. Adolphe Jullien, Berlioz's first biographer worthy of the name, has been my trusty guide. That gentleman's "Hector Berlioz, Sa Vie et ses Œuvres," Paris, 1888, is a perfect mine of information. He has performed with a singular acuteness the task of sifting evidence, and of unravelling the tangled skeins of truth—a task difficult at all times, but made a thousand times more difficult in this instance by the hero himself. Berlioz's "Memoirs" is a fascinating book, but as untrustworthy as fascinating, written originally as a newspaper *feuilleton* and with sensation for its first and supreme object. The facts are surrounded by a sea of fiction, *rari nantes in gurgite vasto*, as Berlioz's favourite author would have said. The chronology of the book is a model of confusion; incidents are misplaced in time and twisted about, and occasionally (that one is compelled to say so!) of deliberate purpose. Yet the memoirs have been slavishly followed, and accepted as apostolic truth by many biographers. Hippeau, in his "Berlioz Intime," was the first to apply the critical scalpel to these *disjecta membra*. Legouvé in his reminiscences has also elucidated many obscure points; but M. Jullien's work is far ahead of either, both as regards the mass of materials and the method of arrangement. In addition to setting old facts right, he has discovered no end of new ones. Berlioz's life in Paris is carefully traced step by step, and M. Jullien, aided by Richard Pohl's valuable researches, has followed his hero to Germany, and even to Russia. Only in one respect the book is singularly wanting. Berlioz's visits to this country are disposed of in as many lines as they ought to have pages, and even the scanty information vouchsafed is not free from serious blunders. The difficulties of our language, our insular position, and, with the exception of Mr. Bennett's well-designed, but of its nature, limited biographical primer, the almost total absence of preliminary local research were evidently insuperable impediments to this French author. The gulf left by him I have tried to fill up very much in his own manner, relying chiefly upon contemporary evidence written, and, where the memory of surviving friends made it possible, oral. The copious notes and extracts from the newspapers which Dr. Freemantle of Sheffield has kindly placed at my disposal, have been of the greatest service to me, and I frankly acknowledge my obligation to him for many extracts from old newspapers which I should have had to find out for myself instead of merely verifying them.

After having traced at some length the preparations which Berlioz made, and which life made for him, in anticipation of his journey to England, it will now be necessary to see how that country itself was prepared to receive the distinguished visitor, and the message he had to deliver. Musical reputations, except in the case of virtuosi and prima-donnas, travelled slowly in those days, and Berlioz had acquired considerable fame on the Continent before the English press, which had scarcely yet developed the musical critic proper, took much notice of him.

As far as I have been able to ascertain, it was not till early in the forties that even the papers more especially concerned with music realised the rise of a new and important power. *The Musical World* of March 9, 1843, contains the following paragraph: "It is rumoured that M. Berlioz, the highly-prized French composer is preparing a new Symphony for the Philharmonic Society, which, it is said, he will conduct in person." This was evidently what, in journalistic phrase, is called a "feeler," for there is no evidence that the Philharmonic directors had any such revolutionary purpose. On April 6 the same information is again repeated in an even more definite form; it is said: "This popular French composer, who several years since married Miss Smithson, the actress, is shortly expected to produce one of his Symphonies in London, having accepted an engagement to that effect from the directors of the Philharmonic Concerts." "Are we to have Berlioz this year at the Philharmonic?" the same paper asks again in November, 1843, alluding probably to the following spring; but neither in 1844, nor at any subsequent period, did the Philharmonic Society go out of its way to do honour to Berlioz. In the meanwhile, other voices chimed in with that of Mr. Davison, who, be it said to his honour, was amongst the first and staunchest advocates of Berlioz, although, from his general bias of taste, it may be surmised that his sympathy was with the man rather than with the music; or perhaps it would be more correct to say, that he liked the music better than he would otherwise have done because the man's talk was so clever and fascinating. *The Morning Post* in May, 1844, speaks of "that wonderful scherzo, 'Queen Mab,' in his 'Romeo and Juliet' Choral Symphony, a work that ought to be heard in this country, if only for the curiosity of hearing how a French musician interprets Shakespeare." The following extract also deserves quotation as one of the rare instances of correct prophecy eight years before the event: "It is positively stated," writes *The Musical World* in November, 1844, "there will be a New Philharmonic Society next season, and amongst the gentlemen already insured as members the name of Berlioz figures prominently."

Berlioz, who was keenly alive to the value of newspaper notoriety, was only too glad to familiarise the English public with his name, and the musical critic of *The Morning Post* having been charged with imitating the French master's criticism of Félicien David's *Le Désert*, he hastened to address the following letter to *The Morning Post*, which appeared in that journal on April 26, 1845:

Sir,
    I have read in an English journal an accusation of plagiarism brought against you with reference to an article on the "Desert" of Félicien David. I could find in the article of the *Morning Post* no trace whatever of that of the *Débats*, and if we agree in our opinion of this work, our manner of expressing it is widely different. I hasten to address you this declaration, and am happy to have the opportunity of expressing to you my sentiments of high esteem and good brotherhood.
                                            Hector Berlioz.

The summons which brought Berlioz to this country was due finally to neither the new nor the old Philharmonic Society, but to the enterprise of an individual. Louis Antoine Jullien, the king of promenade concerts, lives still in the memory of middle-aged people as one of the most imposingly grotesque phenomena of English concert-rooms. His "Allied Armies' Quadrille," his "Indian Quadrille and Havelock's March," and numerous other pieces of the same kind, struck the iron of popular excitement at the moment when it was hottest, and under their convoy Jullien, who, albeit a gigantic humbug, was a lover of good music, managed to smuggle a great many excellent works into public favour. Beginning with detached movements of Symphonies, and finally going so far as to introduce sometimes two complete works of that class in a single concert programme, he did an immense deal for the spread of musical taste in this country, and the artists he engaged were a combination of all the talents. But by far the most striking feature of his concerts was M. Jullien himself. Let us quote Sir George Grove's picturesque description of the man:

In front of this "mass of executive ability," "the Mons"—to adopt the name bestowed on him by *Punch*, whose cartoons have preserved his image with the greatest exactness—with coat thrown widely open, white waistcoat, elaborately embroidered shirt-front, wristbands of extravagant length turned back over his cuffs, a wealth of black hair, and a black moustache—itself a startling novelty—wielded his bâton, encouraged his forces, repressed the turbulence of his audience with indescribable gravity and magnificence, went through all the pantomime of the British Army or Navy Quadrille, seized a violin or piccolo at the moment of climax, and at last sank exhausted into his gorgeous velvet chair. All pieces of Beethoven's were conducted with a jewelled bâton, and in a pair of clean kid gloves, handed him at the moment on a silver salver.

What was it that attracted Jullien to Berlioz? There was no doubt a kind of electric affinity between the two men. Alas that one should have to own it, there was in Berlioz's as well as in Jullien's nature a considerable leaven of the *poseur*. There is something extremely tragic in the fact, but it is a fact nevertheless, that Berlioz with the highest ideals of art ever aspired to by man, was occasionally compelled to stoop to low things. Monster concerts with no artistic object of an appreciable kind, formed part of his programme; and the creator of the "Scène d'Amour" in *Romeo and Juliet*, perhaps the divinest song of love ever conceived by human heart, was also the author of "Le Chant des chemins de fer, grand chœur avec solo de ténor, composé sur des paroles de Jules Janin, et exécuté à Lille pour l'inauguration du chemin de fer du nord (14 Juin, 1846)."

In August, 1847, *la France Musicale* made the startling statement that Hector Berlioz had been engaged by Jullien as the conductor of the English Opera season at Drury Lane, and *The Musical*

World, commenting upon that statement, added: "We are informed Berlioz was on the point of accepting (at the hands of MM. Rocqueplan and Duponchel) an engagement as conductor at the Academy (Paris), when Jullien proffered him, with magnificent terms, the post of conductor at the London theatre, which was instantly accepted." As usual, Jullien had planned his campaign on the largest scale. The orchestra, according to Berlioz's own account, was superb, and the chorus consisted of 120 voices. "Jullien," says an English newspaper, "has engaged the twin poet-librettists, MM. Royer and Vaez, to write six poems, three of which will be put to music by Halévy, Benedict, and Berlioz. In addition to the three-act opera which Jullien has engaged Berlioz to write, he has secured his services to direct four concerts composed of his. (Berlioz's) works."

It is doubtful whether in spite of these allurements Berlioz would have accepted the London engagement, had it not been for two cogent reasons, one public, one personal. Rocqueplan and Duponchel, the managers of the Grand Opéra already named, had played him an extremely shabby trick. They had received the appointment entirely through the influence of Berlioz's patron and employer, M. Bertin, the proprietor of the *Journal des Débats*, and on the understanding that Berlioz was not only to be the conductor, but to have his opera *La Nonne Sanglante* performed without delay. When, however, the papers were signed, these shifty gentlemen adopted a very different tone and placed all manner of difficulties in Berlioz's way. In such circumstances the Drury Lane engagement was particularly gratifying, and accepted without any inquiry into Jullien's capability of carrying out his splendid promises. The second reason appears from a passage in one of the master's letters to his friend the Tajan-Progé of St. Petersburg. Berlioz writes from London, November 10, 1847 : " Je suis venu *seul* à Londres ; vous pouvez en diviner les raisons, d'ailleurs, j'avais un prodigieux besoin de cette liberté qui m'a toujours et partout manqué jusqu'ici. Il a fallu non pas un coup d'état, mais bien une succession de coups d'état pour parvenir à la reprendre." The person of whose presence Berlioz wished to be rid was, it need scarcely be said, not his poor wife, from whom he was separated, but Mdlle. Recio, with whom he found it as difficult to live at this time, as later on when their union had been legalised.

Berlioz arrived in London on November 6, 1847, and went straight to 76 (now 27), Harley Street, where Jullien had provided sumptuous lodgings for his conductor, in the same house where the Beethoven Quartet Society at that time gave its performances. Berlioz, in the " Soirées de l'Orchestre," gives an account of how, by opening his door, he was able to listen to an excellent performance of one of Beethoven's quartets by Ernst, Cooper, Hill, and Rousselot, and how he exclaimed in stentorian tones, " John, shut the door," when the C minor quartet ceased, and a prima donna began to warble. He was also very much struck by observing a number of amateurs following the work in the score, and conceived a high notion of English musical proficiency, until, sitting behind one of these enthusiasts, he noticed that the eyes of the amateur were fixed on page 4, when the executants had arrived at page 6. Altogether his observations on English musicians and English music-lovers are of a very shrewd and pertinent kind, and perhaps a more striking remark on the general attitude of the English public of those, and partly of our own days, has never been made than when Berlioz says that "le désir d'aimer la musique est au moins réel et persistant en Angleterre." In short, Berlioz soon felt at home in England, and in that respect had the advantage of both Liszt and Wagner, who remained strangers in our midst. His English wife and his love of English literature now stood him in good stead. He was able to sympathise with English moods and English life, and when he did criticise, criticised discriminately and leniently. Another advantage was that he had by this time become tolerably familiar with our language, and could communicate with his orchestra without an interpreter. I have been assured by various competent witnesses, that although Berlioz preferred to speak French, he could speak English fluently and even eloquently when it came to the point.

Of his every-day life in London he has himself given lively descriptions in various portions of his letters and memoirs. What struck him most was the terrific hurry of London existence, which made it almost impossible for musicians to concentrate their minds on any particular task. The distances appeared enormous even to a Parisian, and he complains bitterly of the time taken up by paying calls and receiving calls; but he had, from the first almost, a large circle of friends in England, and that circle naturally increased with every new visit. Mr. Osborne and Mr. Ella he had known in Paris, and his warm friendship for them is proved by the letters, since published, which he addressed to them. One of them, written to Mr. Ella, contains the amusing story of how *L'Enfance du Christ* came to be fathered on Pierre Ducré, a musician of the olden time. With Sainton, his compatriot and warm admirer, he naturally lived in daily intercourse, and it was at his house that in 1855 he met Wagner, and formed those pleasant relations which, alas, were not found proof against professional jealousy later on.

Of the English press and its representatives, the French master's experience was of the most pleasant kind. Mr. Davison, as has already been said, took up his cause from the first, and the leader of the critics of those days was followed by most of the other writers of the press, including Mr. Chorley, of *The Athenæum*, and Mr. Gruneisen; and Berlioz was positively delighted with the treatment he had received at the hands of the English newspapers, and which so favourably differed from the attitude of the French critics. M. d'Ortigue, his staunch adherent and colleague on the *Journal des Débats*, is admonished more than once to take note of these "dithyrambes comme on n'en écrivit jamais sur moi," and to "boil them down" into an article for the *Débats*. Only "un vieux niais du *Morning Chronicle*," and later on Mr. Hogarth, whose disapprobation Berlioz charitably attributes to his appointment as Secretary of the old Philharmonic Society, were the chief dissentient voices in a chorus of praise which accompanied Berlioz during his stay in England, with almost unbroken harmony. English critics are sometimes charged with narrow-mindedness and obtuse indifference to new merit, and it is pleasant to cite so striking an exception to the supposed rule. That society, in the ordinary sense of the word, did much for the French composer I have not been able to discover. He visited at Lady Blessington's house, and at Mrs. Grote's, where all the foreign musicians seeking refuge from the French Revolution of 1848 met with kindness and hospitality. The Earl of Westmoreland also sent him a free admission to the Antient Concerts, a courtesy which Berlioz no doubt highly appreciated. But as a rule his acquaintance seems to have chiefly been with literary men and artists. Naturally the stage attracted much of his attention, and he speaks in terms of highest praise of Macready's acting in Sir Henry Taylor's *Philip van Artevelde*, without, however, vouchsafing a single word of commendation to that remarkable work. His attention was evidently entirely absorbed by the stage management, and especially by the grouping of masses, which he describes as superb. He also became personally acquainted with Macready, whom probably he knew from the old Paris days, and who gave him a magnificent dinner in his honour. "C'est un homme charmant, et point du tout prétentieux dans son intérieur," says Berlioz. A friend also put down his name as an honorary member of one of the leading clubs, the atmosphere of which he found extremely oppressive: "Mais Dieu sait le divertissement qu'on peut trouver dans un club anglais!"

I have tried in the above to give a general sketch of Berlioz's life in London during his five visits to this country. It is time that we should return to the chronological order of things.

Berlioz's engagement with Jullien was to the effect that the former was to conduct all the operas, and in addition to this give four grand concerts of his own compositions at an aggregate salary of 20,000 francs. The rehearsals began immediately after his arrival in London, and the first performance of the English Opera season at Drury Lane took place on December 6, 1847. It consisted of Beethoven's *Leonora* Overture, "conducted by Berlioz, who is deeply versed in the scores of Beethoven, with wonderful animation," and this great work formed, curiously enough, the prologue to Donizetti's *Lucia*, called in the English version *The Bride of Lammermoor*. Berlioz detested modern Italian music, and what his feelings may have been when Jullien first revealed the programme of the season to him, one can only vainly imagine. In his letters he speaks of nothing but the great success which the performance had met with; of the five recalls "avec frénésie," granted to Madame Dorus-Gras, the soprano, and Sims Reeves, the tenor, and of the splendid reception given to himself by the public. "Sims Reeves," he says, "has a pretty, natural voice, and he sings as well as that terrible English language will allow any one to sing"—that the terrible English language was that of Shakespeare and his beloved Moore he forgot for the moment. Again he writes: "Reeves is a priceless discovery for Jullien; he has a charming voice, of refined and sympathetic timbre, he is an excellent musician, his face is very expressive, and he acts with the fire of his Irish nationality." (Mr. Reeves, as a matter of fact, was born at Woolwich.)

With the press notices, also, Berlioz expresses himself delighted, and he does not, as he was prone to do, exaggerate; for all the criticisms that I have seen are highly favourable, and the English verdict was summed up in the sentence: " Berlioz has established his continental fame as one of the greatest living conductors." *The Bride of Lammermoor* was repeated several times pending the great event of the season, the production of Balfe's new opera, *The Maid of Honour*, which took place on December 20, 1857, Mr. Sims Reeves again singing the tenor part. The first three performances were, by permission of Mr. Lumley, conducted by Balfe himself, " since when his place has been efficiently occupied by Berlioz who, by his courteous manners and general kindness, has entirely won the affections of the orchestra." The opera does not seem to have had any great success, although in the course of January it was given no less than eighteen times; *Linda di Chamouni* making up the *répertoire*.

That Berlioz's great power was entirely wasted on this kind of music, and that he himself was fully aware of the fact, appears from his confidential correspondence, although he was too good a diplomatist to breathe a word of it in England. Financial troubles were added to the artistic misery of the situation. Jullien's attempt at establishing the English music-drama on a solid basis proved an utter failure; he had opened the theatre without possessing so much as a single piece of music, and with the exception of Balfe's opera, specially written for him, he had to borrow scores and parts from Mr. Lumley. The extraordinary shifts he devised to retrieve his position are humorously described by Berlioz in one of the "Soirées de l'Orchestre." *Robert the Devil* was to be mounted and rehearsed in six days; and when the general rehearsal of *Linda di Chamouni* was called, it was found that there was not a single part on any of the desks. This way of going on, Berlioz adds, is highly characteristic of operatic managers in England. On one side of the Channel they take ten days to mount an opera, which on the other it takes ten months to prepare; and what is worse, the public is perfectly satisfied as long as there are some celebrated names in the cast. The "star system," it would seem, was as rife in 1848 as it is in this present year of grace.

It was probably to pacify his ill-used conductor that Jullien suddenly developed a great admiration for Gluck, one of Berlioz's favourite idols. A model performance of *Iphigenia in Tauris* was to be given, and a committee meeting for devising the best means of effecting that purpose was held at Drury Lane Theatre, on December 14, 1847, Sir Henry Bishop, Berlioz, Planché, Chorley, and Jullien being present. This meeting also Berlioz has described with grim humour. Needless to add that, like the projected performance of *Robert le Diable*, the scheme came to nothing.

In the meantime, Jullien's affairs were going from bad to worse. As early as January 14, that is, less than six weeks after the opening of the theatre, conductor and soloists were without their salaries; the available cash being paid over to chorus, orchestra, and stage carpenters, in order to prevent a strike. Jullien himself had gone to the provinces to give highly successful promenade concerts, and had taken the best instrumentalists with him. He also had sold his publishing business in Regent Street for £8,000. But all this was as a drop in the ocean of the manager's vast liabilities, and the beginning of the end was within measurable distance. Berlioz nevertheless kept up his spirits; he had made up his mind that the recent death of Mendelssohn had opened a splendid chance for a new composer in England, and with that object in view he pushed on the rehearsals for his first concert with feverish energy. That concert took place at Drury Lane Theatre on February 7, 1848, and it may interest the reader to see the programme in full:

Part I.

Overture: "Carnival of Rome."
Romance: "The Young Shepherd" (words by M. De Vere) . Miss Miran.
"Harold in Italy" Symphony, in four parts, with Solo on Tenor, played by Mr. Hill.
1. Harold in the Mountains — Scenes expressive of Melancholy, Happiness, and Joy.
2. March of Pilgrims, singing their Evening Prayer.
3. The Mountaineer of the Abbruzzi to his Mistress.
4. Serenade — Souvenirs of the foregoing Scenes — Revels of Brigands.

Part II.

The First and Second Acts of the Lyrical Drama of "Faust."

Part III.

Cavatina : " Benvenuto Cellini."

Chorus of Souls in Purgatory—"Requiem."

Funeral Oration and Apotheosis; being the Finale of the "Triumphal" Symphony, composed for Double Orchestra and Chorus, expressly by order of the French Government on the removal of the remains of the victims of July, and on the inauguration of the Column of the Bastille.

The artistic success of the concert was greater than the pecuniary one. "His reception," says *The Dramatic and Musical Review*, "throughout the evening must have been gratifying to him. . . . He kept his forces together with a firm hand, and there was but one defection in the chorus throughout the evening. The effect of the entertainment (although the house was crowded with orders) must be to stamp M. Berlioz as a composer of original and effective music." A very interesting article on this concert, by Mr. Edward Holmes, appeared in *The Atlas*, an influential newspaper of those days.

The operatic season at Drury Lane still continued to drag on a precarious existence. On February 9 Mr. Sims Reeves's benefit took place under somewhat stormy conditions. Berlioz's "Carnaval Romain" was played before the opera; then a long delay occurred because Madame Dorus-Gras, probably for financial reasons, refused to perform, and the audience became very riotous indeed, when "just as the storm was at its utmost height, M. Hector Berlioz walked into the orchestra, and his presence turned the tide immediately from exasperation to commendation." On February 16 *The Maid of Honour* was given for the last time by command of the Queen, and on the 20th of the same month the season was prematurely brought to a close with *The Marriage of Figaro*.

Berlioz's occupation as an operatic conductor was now gone, and his high hopes, founded upon Jullien's splendid promises, were crushed in the bud. But he was not easily daunted, and his expectations of a lucrative position in England as the inheritor of Mendelssohn's position were as sanguine as ever. To remain on the spot and keep himself *en évidence* appeared to him a matter of the utmost importance, and he was accordingly a constant frequenter of concerts and all manner of musical celebrations. On February 22 the Royal Society of Musicians gave its annual dinner at the Freemasons' Hall, and among the toasts proposed during the evening was one " containing a just tribute of respect to M. Hector Berlioz, who was invited as a guest. This toast was received with unanimous and long-continued plaudits. M. Berlioz, returning thanks in the French language, paid several compliments to the musical taste and feeling of the English nation, and expressed himself highly flattered by his reception in this country, and gratified by the manner in which his works had been executed by our artists." On March 13 he was present at the first Philharmonic Concert of the season, when Mendelssohn's Italian Symphony was performed. Writing to Mr. Davison, he says: "I was looking for you everywhere the other night, at the Philharmonic Concert. I wished to tell you what you know as well as I—that the Symphony of Mendelssohn is a masterpiece struck at one blow, like a gold medallion. Nothing more new, more vivid, more noble, more learned, has proceeded from his free inspiration. The *Conservatoire* of Paris has not even an idea that this magnificent composition exists! and will discover it about ten years hence."

Persons inclined to suspect a sop to the great critical Cerberus in this emphatic eulogy of his favourite composer would be signally mistaken. With a generosity very rare amongst artists, Berlioz on all occasions expressed unbounded admiration for Mendelssohn, in spite of the ill-disguised contempt for his own music felt and given utterance to by the German master. With regard to the same Italian Symphony, he writes in terms of equal enthusiasm to his intimate friend D'Ortigue, placing it infinitely above " celle également en *la* qu'on joue à Paris," the latter being evidently the Scotch Symphony, which by most people, myself included, is looked upon as Mendelssohn's masterpiece in the highest walk of orchestral art.

On March 28 Berlioz was present at the *matinée*

of the Musical Union at Willis's Rooms, and on April 7 he conducted the "Hungarian March" at a concert of the Amateur Musical Society, when he was enthusiastically received and the March encored. His great desire was to obtain a footing at the Philharmonic Concerts, and with this view another "feeler" was put forth by the friendly *Musical World:*

> We have heard that Mr. Costa, with true liberality and artistic feeling, has proposed to the Philharmonic Society to devote an act of one of the forthcoming concerts to compositions of Berlioz, and has nobly offered to resign the bâton on that occasion. . . . One thing is certain, the Philharmonic Society, in deference to its own responsible position, cannot allow Hector Berlioz to leave London without taking advantage of his presence to give their subscribers a concert of unusual attractions.

For the present this urgent appeal remained a *brutum fulmen*, and before many days were over Berlioz had left London. His departure took place in the second week of July, although I am not able to give the exact date; but before bidding a temporary good-bye to England, he addressed a letter to the editor of *The Musical World*, expressing his gratitude, and hinting, at the same time, that that gratitude was synonymous with "lively anticipation of favours still to receive."

> Mr. Editor,
>   Permit me to have recourse to your journal, as the one which occupies itself exclusively with musical matters, to express in a few words sentiments very natural after the reception I have met with in London.

I am going to return into that country which is still called France, and which, after all, is my own. I am going to see by what means an artist can live, or how long it will take him to die, in the midst of the ruins underneath which the flower of his art is crushed and buried. But, however long the torture which awaits me may endure, I shall preserve till the end the most grateful remembrance of your excellent and skilful artists, of your intelligent and attentive public, and your brethren of the press, who have lent me so noble and so constant a support. I am doubly happy to have been able to admire in them the fine qualities of kindness, talent, and intelligent attention united to the probity of criticism; they are the evident indexes of a veritable love of music, and ought to reassure all the friends of that poor great art on its prospects, by affording them the conviction that you will not allow it to perish. The personal question is, therefore, only secondary here, for you may believe me, that I love *music* much more than *my music,* and I wish that the opportunity of proving it had been oftener given me.

Yes, our muse, terrified by all the horrible clamours which resound from one end of the Continent to the other, seems to me secure of an asylum in England,* and the hospitality will be all

---

* At one time Berlioz thought that asylum jeopardised even in this peaceful island. His "Memoirs" were partly written, or at least put into book form, during his stay in England, and in one of its entries, dated April 10, 1848, the day of the Chartist manifestation, he says: "Perhaps in a few hours England will also be given to confusion, like the rest of Europe, and even this asylum will no longer exist for me." But, at eight o'clock in the evening of the same day, he adds: "After all, those Chartists are a very mild sort of revolutionaries, everything went off well, the guns, those powerful orators, those great logicians, whose irresistible arguments penetrate the masses so deeply, were in the Speaker's seat, but they were not obliged to speak. The mere look of them sufficed to bring to every soul the conviction of the inopportuneness of a revolution, and the Chartists dispersed in the most perfect order. Excellent people! you understand about revolutions as much as the Italians do about the writing of Symphonies!"

the more splendid the more frequently the host remembers that one of his sons is the greatest of poets, that music is one of the diverse forms of poetry, and that on the same liberty which Shakespeare used in his immortal conceptions, depends the entire development of the music of the future.

Adieu, then, all you who have so cordially treated me; my heart is oppressed in quitting you, and I repeat involuntarily, those sad and solemn words of Hamlet's father:

"Farewell, farewell, remember me."

HECTOR BERLIOZ.

This letter, and another of similar purport addressed not long afterwards to *The Morning Post*, give a tolerably correct view of the situation. Berlioz had some cause for gratitude. Although looked upon by the general public, perhaps, more as a strange meteor than as a star of definable magnitude, he had no doubt struck the popular fancy, and critics and more enlightened amateurs looked upon him decidedly as the coming man. His compositions also were beginning to make headway, and Messrs. Cramer & Beale advertised a four-hand arrangement of the "Hungarian March" from *Faust*, and "in the press other works and arrangements by this distinguished composer." No wonder that Berlioz, on his part, thought well of the musical aptitude of the English people, extolling the "fine voices, very common in England," and the "sustained attention of the play and concert-going public." In short, when he left this country in July, 1848, it was fully recognised by himself and others that he was the champion of the progressive party in England, and that, if a great occasion should arise, he would be the man for it.

III.

That occasion was not long in coming, although it had not yet arrived in the last week of May, 1851, when Berlioz visited this country for the second time. He came on this occasion in an official rather than in an artistic capacity. The Great Exhibition was in full swing, and he was appointed a member of the musical jury. He did not again occupy his old lodgings at the Beethoven Rooms, but took a lodging at 27, Queen Anne Street, Cavendish Square. His time was fully taken up by his official duties and by his letters to the *Journal des Débats;* the latter occupation, although always distasteful to him, yielding more satisfactory results.

It is to this period that belong two magnificent specimens of descriptive writing: the one deals with the Crystal Palace at seven o'clock in the morning, the vast building being perfectly still and empty, expectant, as it were, of the crowds from the four quarters of the globe which soon will throng its aisles. The sentiment is essentially that of Wordsworth's famous sonnet on London Bridge:

> Ah, that mighty heart is lying still,

although Berlioz had probably never heard of that masterpiece of English sonnet writing. The other article (both are now embodied in "Les Soirées de l'Orchestre") echoes the profound impression which the voices of 6,000 charity children singing in unison at St. Paul's had made upon the master of grand effects. Berlioz stood amongst the choristers clad in a surplice, and joining in the chanting of the Psalms as well as his emotion would allow him. On leaving the great church he met old Cramer, who, forgetting in his transports of delight that he could speak French, kept calling out in Italian : " Cosa stupenda! stupenda! la gloria dell' Inghilterra !" Duprez, the great tenor, was also present, and also in tears. I may mention that Berlioz was present again at the anniversary meeting of the charity schools in the next following year. *The Musical World* of June 3, 1852, writes : " Among the choir were observed, in surplices, Berlioz, Joachim, Osborne," etc.

His labours on the jury were probably not of a very agreeable kind. Berlioz has described the troubles of a musical umpire in connection with another exhibition ; and eager tradesmen and manufacturers are the same all the world over. The musical jury, Class X., consisted of many distinguished members, including Sir Henry Bishop (Chairman), Sir George Smart, Thalberg, Berlioz, the Chevalier Neukomm, Cipriani Potter, Dr. Wylde, and Sterndale Bennett. But in spite of this, one of the papers somewhat rudely remarks that, "the jury, as ultimately settled, contained but one man, and him a foreigner—Berlioz—who could be said to possess any extensive knowledge of musical instruments, and even in his case scientific attainment was wanting;" and the same journal remarks of the official report, "that a more miserably weak and worthless document never appeared on a great public occasion." Nevertheless the French master's second visit to England, which came to a close in the last week of July, was not without important results; for it was, no doubt, between, and perhaps at, the official jury-meetings that he and Dr. Wylde discussed a scheme, the consummation of which startled the world not many months afterwards.

IV.

The foundation of the New Philharmonic Society in 1852, raised expectations, and was greeted by contemporaries with a chorus of hopeful joy which subsequent events did not altogether justify. The old Philharmonic Society, which at that time had almost the monopoly of orchestral music in London, used or abused its position in the manner peculiar to monopolists. New music was rare in its programmes; it clung to the so-called classical masters with a tenacity doubly accounted for by the fossilised taste of its patrons, and by the fact that familiar works might be performed with some credit even after the one rehearsal which, monstrous to relate, was all that was allowed for each concert. Even Mendelssohn's genius had been unable to rouse the Philharmonic from its slumbers, during his one year of office; and when Wagner came to be confronted with the so-called traditions of this orchestra, in 1855, he shrewdly surmised that Mendelssohn, having found reform impossible, meekly acquiesced in existing evils. "By the Philharmonic Society," remarked a not malevolent critic, "the works of Berlioz, though of European fame, have been studiously avoided, simply because they imperatively demand the most careful rehearsal."

Intelligent musicians of all parties felt at last that this state of things was intolerable, and that the only possible remedy lay in competition. To Dr. Wylde belongs the credit of having brought these vague aspirations to a point, and in having concentrated the necessary energies, and raised the necessary funds for the foundation of a rival institution which was appropriately called the New Philharmonic Society. The prospectus of that Society, issued in January, 1852, and signed by Mr. Beale, its secretary, is a curious document. Starting from the general proposition that the "faithful performance of a fine composition is an ever-springing source of pleasure," it defines the mission of the new Society in the following sentences, pompously expressed, but full of true meaning withal:

The New Philharmonic Society has for its object the diffusion and advancement of Musical Art. It is proposed not only to extend a knowledge of the productions of the greatest masters by a more perfect performance of their works than has hitherto been attained, but likewise to give to modern and native composers a favourable opportunity for establishing the worth of their claims upon the attention and esteem of a discerning public. Exclusiveness, the baneful hindrance to all progress of art, will not be tolerated in this society. To exclude works of living authors because they have not the excellencies of the illustrious dead, is as absurd as to deny the advantages of the discovery of new countries because they do not possess the civilisation and beauties of ancient Rome or Greece. Some degree of novelty must be one of the materials of every instrument which works upon the mind, and curiosity blends itself more or less with all the passions. "The first and the simplest emotion," says Burke, "which we discover in the human mind, is curiosity." Now, while on the one hand, by a performance of new works, laudable curiosity is gratified, on the other hand encouragement is given to unknown and aspiring talent, while a better appreciation of the excellence of former works is imparted to the public. Modern works may not approach the perfection of those of a former period; yet they will bear a peculiarity of style, an impress of manner, will be tinted with the complexion of the present age, and may thus convey a charm which earlier works, however superior, cannot possess.

When *entrepreneurs* begin to talk about Greece and Rome, and cite Burke and other authorities, their words generally rouse suspicions in experienced bosoms. But that the Philharmonic directors meant what they somewhat magniloquently expressed, was sufficiently proved by their appointing Berlioz as their conductor and by giving him *carte blanche* in the matter of rehearsals. As to this point, Berlioz expresses himself with wonder and delight, adding that the directors neither expected nor desired immediate gain; Mr. Beale, who, albeit a tradesman, was a genuine lover of music, declaring publicly that the rehearsals for Beethoven's Choral Symphony alone had swallowed up more than a third of the entire subscription. "Do not tell this in France," Berlioz cautiously adds in the letter to D'Ortigue, where the message occurs.

The opening concert took place at Exeter Hall on March 24, 1852, and the success was, according to Berlioz, pyramidal. "I was recalled," he adds, "more times than I can remember, and acclaimed both as a composer and conductor." The press the next morning was again, according to Berlioz, dithyrambic in its praise, and it must be owned that, in this instance, he only slightly exaggerates. The papers that I have consulted are unanimous in their more or less qualified approbation, and even " le vieux niais du *Chronicle*" had by this time either been superseded or mended his manner. "The character of the music," that journal says, speaking of the "Romeo and Juliet" Symphony, which, with the omission of the Finale, was given at the beginning of the second part, "is wild, passionate, and perfectly original in its piquancy of treatment, particularly as regards the wooden band. The ideas are worked out in a thoroughly dramatic manner, and there runs through the whole an unfailing vein of imagination, sometimes bright and sparkling, and again plaintively and passionately sombre." It is true that this critic was not over pleased with the reading of the "Jupiter" Symphony, which opened the concert; but Berlioz might console himself with *The Times*, which "had never heard a more perfect execution of Mozart's magnificent Symphony," although "the omission of the repeats was a double mistake, a mistake of taste and a mistake of policy." Mozart's work was followed by a selection from *Iphigenia in Tauris*, Berlioz still remaining faithful to the idol of his youth, and Beethoven's "Triple" Concerto (Messrs. Silas, Sivori, and Piatti), and Weber's "Oberon" Overture completed the first part. The "Song of Thoas" in the Gluck fragment was, curiously enough, sung by all the male choristers, a strange proceeding on behalf of so ardent a purist as Berlioz, for which *The Athenæum* takes him roundly to task; not without a show of justice. But the audience, caring no more about purism in those than it does in our days, encored it.

As to the "Romeo and Juliet" Symphony, *The Times* is most outspoken in its praise, and its highly pertinent remarks do great credit to the critic, and are well worth reading even in our day, when the work is much more generally acknowledged to be a masterpiece than it was thirty-six years ago.

That M. Berlioz has a poetical mind, that he has in him much of the quality of a painter, that he is wholly independent of mere conventionalities, that he disdains commonplace, that he aspires to raise himself up to his subject, and that he tries to invent, if he does not positively succeed in finding, something entirely new on his own account, we cannot suppose any unprejudiced person who, capable of judging, listened attentively to last night's performance will be prepared to deny. There is an earnestness in the whole of the work which shows the composer to have been full to the brim of his subject. From the quarrels of the Montagues and Capulets, with which the Symphony opens, to the illustration of Queen Mab, with which the first part concludes, there is continued evidence of aspiration, if not of absolute creative genius. This last, as a piece of instrumentation, defies description. The orchestral combinations, as unprecedented as they are often singularly happy, are all exclusively the property of Berlioz, who discovered them, and to whose wild and wayward imagination they are as tints to give variety to his pictures. A more gorgeous example of instrumental colouring than the long movement in A major, which follows the joyous chorus of the Capulet youths reeling home from their orgie, was never written; such an endless change of tone, such ever-shifting gradations, and so nicely balanced and contrasted, could alone render a *morceau* of such unusual length endurable. Berlioz, however, has rendered it not merely endurable but interesting from first to last, and we must venture an opinion that this " Scène d'Amour," as it is entitled in the score, is not only the most beautiful passage in the Symphony of " Romeo and Juliet," but the most gorgeous piece of musical colouring by a musical colourist, whose most vivid scenes must recall to the ardent observer the later pictures which came from the golden brush of Turner.

The Athenæum is more guarded in its remarks, and institutes an elaborate comparison between the play and its attempted musical rendering, in which altogether it discovers more " excellent and shrewd sense " than creative genius; admitting, however, the " charm, glow, tenderness, grandeur " of the orchestral colouring. Regarding the excellence of the performance, in which Miss Dolby sang the contralto and Mr. Lockey the tenor solos, the papers are unanimous, as well as regarding the applause with which it was received. The orchestra was indeed one of singular excellence, and included many names familiar as household words to this day Sivori led the violins, Piatti the violoncelli, Bottesini the double basses (twelve in number), Messrs. C. Harper and Garrett were the two first horns, Mr. T. Harper the first trumpet. Even the *crotales*, or antique cymbals, of the *pianissimo* of which Berlioz speaks with special delight, were in the hands of such artists as M. Silas and Mr. W. Ganz. It throws a curious side light upon the miscellaneous taste and comprehensive appetite of these days if one reads that after such a work the audience were still able to appreciate a Fantasia on the double bass by Signor Bottesini, and Rossini's Overture to *Guillaume Tell*.

So far everything had passed off satisfactorily; the birth of the new Society had attracted no end of attention; and the different opinions expressed only tended to keep the interest alive. But already, at the second concert given on April 14, a note of personal disagreement mingles with the chorus of artistic enthusiasm. This concert was chiefly devoted to the "encouragement of native talent," an expression used in the newspaper criticisms of those days as an epithet of admiration by one party, and of derision by the other. Dr. Wylde contributed a

Pianoforte Concerto in F minor, played by M. Alexandre Billet, and the second part of the concert was mainly taken up by an operatic masque entitled, "The Island of Calypso," by Edward Loder, the composer of the "Night Dancers," in which Mr. and Mrs. Sims Reeves, Miss Dolby and Mr. Weiss took the soli. The performance had not been sufficiently rehearsed, and seems, by all accounts, to have been indifferent; but it was with regard to the soli that the quarrel already alluded to arose. So stringent had been the censure of the press that Berlioz, according to his not very commendable custom, thought it necessary to rush into print, and he accordingly wrote an explanatory letter to Mr. Loder, which was duly published in *The Musical World:*

To Mr. Loder, of Manchester.

Sir,
I think it my duty to offer you some explanations on the subject of the execution of your beautiful work at the second concert of the New Philharmonic Society. You were absent, but be assured I neglected nothing to secure for it a good performance. Some faults, however, by no means numerous, were remarked upon in the execution of the last part. We might have had to deplore more serious accidents. Mr. and Mrs. Reeves, entrusted with the parts of "Telemachus" and "Eucharis," not having been present at a single rehearsal with the orchestra. At the first rehearsal (with wind instruments and double quartet) I was compelled to sing, as well as I could, the airs and recitatives while directing the orchestra. At the second, with eighty musicians, Miss Dolby and Mr. Weiss alone attended. At the third, with the semi-orchestra, in Blagrove's Rooms, I was again obliged to sing the parts of "Eucharis" and "Telemachus," Mr. and Mrs. Reeves being again absent. These two artists have only rehearsed on one

occasion with me, the same day as the concert, and the orchestra in consequence was obliged to accompany them without having heard them. You will understand, therefore, why the band occasionally wanted confidence in the recitatives. Nevertheless, the only grave error we have to regret was not committed by the orchestra. I was on the point of refusing to direct the execution of a work of such importance under such strange conditions; but the fear of having my conduct misconstrued restrained me. It is the first time in my life I was ever placed in such a position. You will see that I was forced to submit to it, and it is only me, I can assure you, whom it has compromised.

Receive, sir, the assurance of my high esteem for your musical merit, and my distinguished sentiments for yourself.

Your all-devoted
HECTOR BERLIOZ.

15th *April*, 1852.

This grave impeachment not unnaturally elicited a retort at once direct and characteristic on the part of the popular tenor. It is amusing to meet, at this early day, with an instance of that indisposition which has played so important a part in Mr. Sims Reeves's career. To that cause he attributes his absence from the second rehearsal, omitting, however, to explain whether Mrs. Sims Reeves, who also failed to put in an appearance, was sympathetically indisposed! Of the first rehearsal he had had no intimation when he left London for a few days, and "of another rehearsal mentioned by M. Berlioz, we heard nothing whatever; this, sir, is my explanation."

The Finale and peroration of this remarkable document is written with a pungency and directness which makes one wonder whether the same hand which penned these lines could possibly have traced the rambling life and recollections, recently published, as "written by himself," by the great tenor; unless, indeed, the burden of years affects the hand more severely than the voice. "Were the *fautes peu nombreuses*, which elicited a chorus of condemnation from the press, committed by us only? Did our non-attendance at rehearsal make the band falter in the recitatives and songs of the other artists? Did it give unsteadiness to the choristers? M. Berlioz says that the only *grave error* was not committed by the orchestra, but with due deference I must observe that it appears to me a very *grave error* to perform a work from first to last without any successful attempt at accent or colouring, and this was certainly the case with the execution of Mr. Loder's 'Calypso,' and will be so whenever a conductor (however exalted his merits) consents to give a new and *bel ouvrage* to the public with only one full band rehearsal."

Apart from Beethoven's C minor Symphony the remainder of the second concert did not contain anything noteworthy, and Berlioz's works shine by their absence. At the third concert (April 28, 1852), on the other hand, the "Romeo and Juliet" was repeated by general desire, and performed, according to the composer, even better than on the first occasion. This concert deserves to be remembered chiefly by two incidents of a personal kind. The pianist was Madame Pleyel, the same person whom, as Mdlle.

Moke, Berlioz had loved, and desired to assassinate, if his own account is true. What were the feelings of Berlioz when brought into personal contact with his old flame he has omitted to state. But the lady, after the manner of her kind, seems to have been less reticent. It appears that the accompaniment to Weber's "Concertstück" was played somewhat roughly; and that particularly in one of the solo passages the orchestra crashed in a bar or two too soon, thus spoiling an effect intended for the pianist. I am positively assured that Madame Pleyel attributed this *contretemps* to the spite of her jilted lover, and complained to several members of the committee. No candid judge will attribute such meanness to the great composer. At the same time, the orchestral playing in the piece in question seems to have been exceptionally bad, and a contemporary writer attributes the pianist's comparative failure in some measure to the carelessness of M. Berlioz, who took no pains to keep the accompaniments within due bounds; so that Madame Pleyel had literally to force her way through that deservedly popular work by dint of her own individual powers.

The second incident was of a more pleasant kind. The widow of Spontini had come over to London for the purpose of hearing the extracts from the *Vestale,* and sent to Berlioz the *bâton* used during his career by her husband, together with the following letter:

Sir,
    I came here to attend the Concert this evening. Will you permit me to present to you the bâton with which my dear husband used to conduct the works of Gluck, Mozart, and his own. It cannot be transmitted to better hands than yours. When you are conducting, this evening, *La Vestale*, it will vividly remind you of my dear husband, who loved and admired you so much. Heaven has refused him the satisfaction of hearing the last performance of his *Olympia* at Berlin, and that of *La Vestale* conducted by you. Yet he will hear you this evening!

By this time the public interest in the proceedings of the New Philharmonic Society had begun somewhat to flag, but it was roused once more to a pitch of enthusiasm by the fourth concert (May 12, 1852), when the Ninth Symphony, at that time little known to English people, was given. As to this performance it is unnecessary to quote newspaper extracts, for it still lives in the memory of many musicians who were present, and who are unanimous in testifying that such singing and such playing had never been heard before and were very rarely heard afterwards in an English concert-room. Berlioz knew the score by heart, and threw his whole soul into its perfect rendering; and his enthusiasm had communicated itself to every man in the orchestra, every singer in the chorus. Seven band rehearsals had been held, and in addition to this, strings and wood, wind and brass, had been put through their paces separately. No wonder, then, that in a technical, as well as in an intellectual sense, the performance was perfect, and in its way monumental. Madame Clara Novello, Miss Williams, Mr. Sims Reeves, and Herr Staudigl, were the solo quartet.

The fifth concert, May 28, was again of less interest, a Pianoforte Concerto by M. Silas being the principal novelty. Berlioz's Overture, "Les Francs Juges," was also performed, and seems to have disappointed the audience. At the sixth and last concert, June 9, the Ninth Symphony was repeated; and a Cantata, "Prayer and Praise," by Dr. Wylde, as well as fragments from Berlioz's "Faust" Cantata, were in the second part of the programme. Madame Pleyel also appeared again, but had taken the precaution to select a piece without orchestral accompaniments. According to *The Musical World*, the "Faust" fragments made a very favourable impression, and Berlioz, in his summing up of the season, is, as usual, full of enthusiasm. "What a thing it was to see the enormous public at Exeter Hall roused by the extracts from 'Romeo' and 'Faust,' to hear the hurrahs of our grand orchestra! I frequently thought of you, my dear Morel, in the evening on coming home, when we had supper with these Englishmen, real enthusiasts, with rum and iced champagne. What a singular, what a grand nation! It understands everything, or at least it contains people who understand everything."

Unfortunately, the people who understood everything, or at least who understood Berlioz, were not numerous enough to make the fortunes of the New Philharmonic Society. The season had no doubt been an artistic success, but it had been a financial failure; and Mr. Beale, Berlioz's chief supporter, who had already some weeks before given him an engagement for the second season, had to cancel that engagement, and to announce his own resignation as secretary of the Society. Berlioz was naturally extremely disappointed, and, according to his wont, attributed the failure to personal spite. In the letter to his friend Morel, already quoted, he says: " One of my *chefs-d'orchestre* has found means to have my engagement cancelled. He has been chaffed (*berné*) during the past year by the artists, the public, and the press so much, that he says he will take his revenge by choosing for next year a partner less unaccommodating than myself. He wants to engage old Spohr. Improving upon this hint, M. Jullien commits himself to the following statement: 'Beale sent in his resignation to the committee because Costa, in alliance with the pianist Dr. Wylde (*sic*), had brought it about that Berlioz should not be engaged, and that in his place either old Spohr or Lindpaintner should be invited, from whom he thought he had nothing to fear as a conductor.'" The substratum of truth in this sentence is that Lindpaintner conducted the first four, and Spohr the two last concerts of the season of 1853, in conjunction with Dr. Wylde. The other statements contained in the same sentence are partly very doubtful, and partly sheer nonsense. Every one knows that Costa had absolutely nothing to do with the management of the New Philharmonic Society, and was from his position the very last person in England to be consulted. As to the resignation of Mr. Beale, which, by the way, seems to have been withdrawn—for the prospectus of the second season is signed by him—it was due mainly, if not exclusively, to financial causes.

The New Philharmonic Society was originally started by four gentlemen—Sir Charles Fox, Mr. Thomas Brassey (the father of the present Lord Brassey), Mr., afterwards Sir Morton Peto, the great railway contractor, and Dr. Wylde, each of whom put down two hundred pounds. Mr. Beale, of Cramer & Co., undertook the general and financial management. That management, as we have already seen, was carried on in an extremely liberal spirit. Any number of rehearsals was allowed to Berlioz, and no expenses were spared for the excellent orchestra engaged by Mr. Jarrett, which had Sivori for its leader, and many of the best artists of the day for its members. The receipts had been generally good, but they were far from equal to such heavy demands. When the balance sheet was presented at the end of the season, it turned out that the original capital had been expended within a few pounds, in addition to which Mr. Beale or his firm were out of pocket for a very considerable sum. The four guarantors were accordingly called upon for nearly the whole amount of their subscription (£102 18s. 6d. was the exact sum), and be it said to the credit of the commercial gentlemen, that they paid their money down without any demur; Mr. Brassey adding that "it would have been much more agreeable to him if the deficiency had been divided by three instead of by four," and if Dr. Wylde, the artistic member of the committee, "had released himself from any deficit." At the same time the committee-meeting was not of a very cheerful kind, and it appears that in consequence of some remarks then made, Mr. Beale sent in his resignation. It was also not unnatural that the New Philharmonic directors should have been anxious to engage for their second season a conductor a little less exacting in the matter of rehearsals, and therefore a little less expensive than Berlioz. That Dr. Wylde was not in any sense hostile to the great French composer is sufficiently proved by the fact that three years later, when he had the sole responsibility of the concerts, he was most anxious to have again the services of Berlioz. I have before me a whole series of letters addressed by Berlioz to Dr. Wylde, and written in the most cordial terms, in which he asks him "non comme à un directeur de concerts, mais comme à un artiste," to be released from his promise to conduct the entire series of concerts of 1855; and he accordingly was present only at the last two. This does not look like ill-will on the one side, or permanent offence on the other.

V.

Berlioz was too accustomed to adversity to be easily daunted, and with Beale's letter before him he speaks of other English plans with unabated hopefulness. "I hear again of a number of new schemes," he writes, "always for England; here, in Paris, always—nothing." The English schemes soon took definite shape; nothing less was intended than a performance at Covent Garden of *Benvenuto Cellini*—the opera which had signally failed in Paris at the Grand Opéra in 1838, but which Liszt had quite recently (March 20, 1852) produced at Weimar with great success. Berlioz's popularity in England at the time was so great, that an equally favourable result might be expected almost with certainty, but the persons who anticipated such a success entirely overlooked the difference which existed and exists in England between those who frequent orchestral concerts, and the *habitués* of the Italian Opera. The fatal consequences of this mistake became apparent when, on Saturday, June 25, 1853, the Italian version of *Benvenuto* saw the light at Covent Garden. If the New Philharmonic Concerts had been Berlioz's Austerlitz, this was his Waterloo. "The performance," writes Mr. Chorley, in his "Thirty Years' Musical Recollections," "was prepared with great care, and the composer himself presided in the orchestra. Mesdames Julienne-Dejean and Nantier-Didiée, and Messrs. Tamberlik, Formes, and Tagliafico taking the principal parts. The evening was one of the most melancholy evenings which I ever passed in any theatre. At an early period the humour of the audience began to show itself, and the painful spectacle had to be endured of seeing the composer conducting his own work through every stage of its condemnation. The Queen and Prince Albert, and the King and Queen of Hanover, were present, but even the presence of these distinguished persons was unable to check the disgraceful conduct of the audience, venting itself in cat-calls and howls louder even than the thunderstorm which was raging outside. An attempt even was made to stop the performance of the overture, 'Carnaval Romain,' which served as an introduction to the second act, and which, together with other compositions by Berlioz, had been applauded less than a month before[*] at one of the Old Philharmonic Concerts at the Hanover Square Rooms." No wonder that, as *The Musical World* briefly states, "the manage-

---

[*] The Concert took place on Monday, May 30, at the Hanover Square Rooms, and the selection from the works of Berlioz, conducted by himself, consisted of "Harold in Italy" (Viola Solo, M. Sainton), "The Repose of the Holy Family" (Signor Gardini), and "Le Carnaval Romain." The second part of the Concert, including Beethoven's C minor Symphony and a miscellaneous selection, was conducted by Costa.

ment did not think it expedient to bring *Benvenuto Cellini* forward again." The press notices of the work and the performance would furnish an interesting study if sufficient space were at hand, and if the reader's patience had not already been tried by too many quotations. The desire of the critics, on the whole, seems to have been to "let down easily" a composer for whom many of them had expressed admiration in public, and whose unfair and dastardly treatment at the hands of the audience all of them could scarcely help condemning. At the same time the opera does not seem to have pleased the critics any more than it did the audience, and even the warmest admirer of Berlioz at this day would scarcely hold it up as a masterpiece, in spite of many detached beauties and glimpses of genius. Never having seen one of his operas on the stage, I am loth to give a definite opinion on the point; but, as far as one can judge by pianoforte arrangements, it seems to me that Berlioz did not possess dramatic genius in the proper sense of the word. His nature was too lyrical, too expansive for that; he lacked the crispness of touch, the succinctness of utterance, the concentration of impulse, which go to the making of a great writer for the stage, apart from which he had no definite and consistent idea of the musico-dramatic form. Much as he despised the fireworks and the meaningless conventionalities of the Italian and light French schools, he employs the same conventionalities in *Benvenuto*, in *Béatrice et Bénédict*, and even in *Les Troyens*, without hesitation, and in close and startling juxtaposition with poetic beauties of a very high order. And it is not, perhaps, matter for much regret that the recent Berlioz revivals in France and England have not led to the mounting of a single one of his operas, although Mr. Rosa at one time announced *Benvenuto* at Her Majesty's Theatre, and had even a statue of Perseus cast for the purpose. I do not mean to deny that an intelligent and artistically-minded manager might and should have made a trial; but I greatly doubt whether such a trial would have redounded much to the credit of Berlioz.

By way of a specimen of contemporary criticism, I add a few sentences from *The Times'* notice of *Benvenuto*, which is written essentially on the lines above indicated, and may be called a model of tact and good feeling.

After stating that the libretto of *Benvenuto Cellini* was among the very worst entrusted to a musical composer, and that M. Berlioz was really to be pitied, *The Times* of June 27, 1853, remarks: " The instrumental prelude to Act II., ' Carnaval Romain,' is a splendid piece of orchestration; and the fact that this was hissed here when it was always applauded elsewhere, must have led many to suspect the entire sincerity of those continued marks of disapproval dealt indiscriminately by a resolute and determined party, at almost every *morceau*, good, bad, and indifferent. . . . That the music of *Benvenuto Cellini* is composed on principles in opposition to those of the acknowledged masters is true. But because a thing is new, that is no proof of its being bad. For our own part, amid much that was objectionable according to the received notions of art which we have always been the first to uphold, we detected much that deserved to be admired. The instrumentation is often unnecessarily intricate and oftener unnecessarily noisy. The cymbals and big drum, except in the 'Carnaval,' are a nuisance, and go far to damage what is otherwise intrinsically fine. The rhythm is often broken and irregular, so as to torment and puzzle the ear; and several of the melodies which begin happily, are spoiled by being tortured into strange and unexpected cadences. The scene of the 'Carnaval,' though full of life and colour, is decidedly too long; and the contortions of the Polichinello, together with the satirical dumb show directed against that very uninteresting personage Balducci, occupy a considerable space of time without offering any attraction to the audience. And yet, there is some excellent music in this scene. All the part which is a repetition from the overture, is striking and characteristic, while the choruses of the people, and their exclamations of pleasure as the piece in the Theatre of Cassandro is being enacted, are picturesque and dramatically appropriate.

Granted that there are many things to offend the prejudices of those who look exclusively to the accepted models of dramatic musical composition, that there is much that sounds prolix and monotonous, that the voices are at times injudiciously taxed, and that there are many odd combinations with a great deal of straining after effects not always obtained, we find on the other hand enough of pleasing, original, and effective to counterbalance these drawbacks, and to entitle *Benvenuto Cellini* to consideration, if not to approval."

A story which does infinite credit to the hearts of the two persons concerned, and which I have on the best authority, may be told in connection with this unfortunate *première*. It appears that Berlioz had asked the principal artists and a few friends to a supper after the performance, to celebrate the anticipated success. When that success was converted into a dismal failure, none of the *convives* liked to put in an appearance, with the sole exception of Mr. Davison. The table was spread for many guests and the two men sat down at the deserted board, Berlioz being moved to tears by the tact and true politeness shown by his solitary guest. The parallel scene from the "Virginians," when George Warrington entertains his friends after the discomfiture of Pocahontas, must have recalled this interesting evening to Mr. Davison's mind when he came to read Thackeray's novel some years later. The amount of sympathy and of lachrymose moisture mixed on both those occasions with the more substantial viands was something prodigious.

It is needless to say that Berlioz attributed his defeat to personal motives, and that the chief leader of the intrigue got up against him assumed in his mind the features of Signor Costa. During his stay in London Berlioz had, so to speak, Costa on the brain. People had been comparing his own conducting with that of the Italian maestro, not to the advantage of the latter. He had himself attacked Costa in the *Journal des Débats;* what, then, was more likely than that the wily Neapolitan should have availed himself of this opportunity of revenging himself upon his rival? It is true, and Berlioz has to acknowledge it, that Costa had been most helpful and serviceable during the rehearsals, but this, Berlioz charitably suggests, might have been a feint to cover a deep-laid design. "Public opinion, if not mine," the master says in his Memoirs, "points in that direction;" and the article in *The Times,* above quoted, certainly hints at the existence of a cabal. Intrinsically it is probable enough that Costa, and the Italians generally, had no particular good-will towards a man who called Bellini a *petit polisson* and made a point of speaking of modern Italian music with the utmost contempt. At the same time, intrinsic evidence is scarcely sufficient to sustain a charge of malice prepense, and it is extremely difficult to bring forward direct testimony in such a case. Certain it is that the loudest clamours of the Italian clique would soon have been silenced by the indignation of the impartial public if *Benvenuto Cellini* had pleased, or if Berlioz's popularity in England had been anything like what he believed it to be. In the theatre itself no dissentient voice was raised, but the friends of the master were naturally eager to make some *amende* to his wounded feelings; Mr. Beale, who had from the beginning been his staunch adherent, again taking the initiative. The first idea was to give a concert for the master's benefit at Exeter Hall; and when this had to be abandoned, owing to his departure from England, the money already collected, to the amount of £200, was offered to him as a free gift. Berlioz at the time was in straitened circumstances, and five thousand francs would have been a most welcome addition to his slender funds; but he thought of what his enemies in Paris would say of his accepting this bounty, and declined with a heavy heart. The English committee then determined upon purchasing the full score of *Faust*, and publishing the same with English words; and this delicate compliment was accepted with gratitude.

"My dear ——," Berlioz wrote, "the concert cannot take place. The gentlemen of the committee organised to get it up have conceived the delicate, charming, and generous idea of devoting the sum realised by the subscription opened for the concert, to the acquisition of the score of my *Faust*, which will be published, with English text, under the superintendence of Beale and other members of the committee. It would be impossible to be more cordial and artist-like at the same time; and I rejoice at the result of the performance at Covent Garden, since it has been the cause of a demonstration so sympathetic, intelligent, and worthily expressed. Give all the publicity in your power to the manifestation; you will render justice to your compatriots, and at the same time confer a very great pleasure on

"Yours, etc.,
"HECTOR BERLIOZ."

Berlioz left England on July 9, and, after a short stay in Paris, went on to Baden, where a grand festival in his honour had been prepared by that somewhat equivocal but ardent admirer of his art, M. Bénazet, the farmer of the gambling tables, by whose commission *Béatrice et Bénédict* was written later on.

VI.

Two years elapsed before he again, and for the last time, trod English ground. By that time considerable changes had taken place in this country. Signor Costa, in December, 1854, resigned the conductorship of the Philharmonic Society, and, at the suggestion of his friend, M. Sainton, the post was offered to Berlioz, who, however, had already been engaged by the New Philharmonic Society. Originally that engagement was for the whole season; but when other and more advantageous proposals were made to him in Germany, he wrote to Dr. Wylde, asking to be released from his promise, and his prayer was granted. The correspondence, to which allusion has already been made, is a voluminous one, and none of the letters having hitherto been published, one of them may be given here as a specimen of Berlioz's mode of expression in the ordinary affairs of life and apart from sentiment:

Mon cher Monsieur Wilde,

Je m'addresse à vous non comme à un directeur de concerts, mais comme à un artiste. Une foule de propositions très avantageuses me sont faites de tous côtés pour la saison prochaine, aux quelles, à cause de la votre, il me sera impossible de répondre affirmativement. Je ne puis manquer à la parole que je vous ai donnée; mais considerez le tort immense que vous allez faire à ma carrière, en m'obligeant à refuser ce qui m'est offert. Soyez assez bon confrère pour me rendre ma parole et ma liberté, je vous en aurai une extrême reconnaissance; il vous sera facile d'ailleurs de me remplacer pour les *deux concerts*. En attendant votre prompte réponse, qui je l'espère, sera favorable, recevez l'assurance de mes sentiments les plus distingués.

Votre tout devoué
H. Berlioz.

17, Rue de Boursault, Paris.
   26 Decembre, 1854.

It was finally settled that Dr. Wylde should conduct the first four, and Berlioz the last two concerts of the season, and he accordingly arrived in London early in June to conduct the rehearsals for the fifth of the six concerts. Wagner by that time had nearly got through his martyrdom at the old Philharmonic Society, and the contemporary press recorded an astonishing fact: Wagner and Berlioz, the two ultra-republicans in the realms of music, installed in the two most prominent posts of the musical world of this classical and exclusively conservative London.

The fifth New Philharmonic Concert was given on Wednesday evening, June 13, and the principal item of the programme was once more the "Romeo and Juliet" selection. The selection on this occasion was confined to orchestral pieces. What had become, by this time, of the splendid chorus of which Berlioz spoke in terms of such praise in 1852? one asks, on reading that at the general rehearsal of June 12 "the vocal portion of 'Romeo and Juliet' was rendered so badly after several trials, that Berlioz decided to omit it." This necessary precaution seems to have riled the chorus singers to an unbearable degree, and when the master entered the orchestra for the second part of the concert, they took the extreme and unprecedented measure of hissing him, while the public, we are told, greeted him with a simultaneous tumult of applause. Even the orchestra seems to have done its duty in a very leisurely fashion, for Wagner, who was present, writes: "The very imperfect execution of his 'Romeo and Juliet' Symphony made me pity him." With Berlioz's reading of the G minor Symphony by Mozart, Wagner was also "little edified;" but *The Musical World* is in raptures with the rendering of Mr. Henry Leslie's overture, "The Templar," saying: "The marked pains bestowed upon it by Berlioz warranted the assumption that the renowned foreign musician was well satisfied to conduct an English composition of such merit." The remainder of the concert was of no special interest.

The conduct of the chorus could, of course, not pass unnoticed, and an angry controversy arose in the press, to which Berlioz, always ready for a newspaper fray, contributed the following letter, addressed to the editor of *The Musical World*:

SIR,
One of the members of the chorus of the New Philharmonic Society demands from me an explanation on the subject of the suppression of the choruses of my Symphony ("Romeo and Juliet") at the concert which I directed at Exeter Hall the 13th of this month. The reasons which compelled me to make the suppression were evident and imperious. The little chorus of the prologue, for fourteen voices only, had been studied *in the French language*, M. and Mdme. Gassier being, to my great astonishment, engaged for the solos of this part of my Symphony, which it was impossible for them to sing in English. Now, at the last moment, M. Gassier, whose voice is a baritone, declared that he could not sing a tenor part, and that Mdme. Gassier (a high soprano) could not sing a contralto part, as was evident to myself. It was then necessary to commence new studies with the English text, and the extremely difficult choruses, the words of which should be well

pronounced, and without any accompaniment, could not be sufficiently learned in so short a time.

As for the song of the Capulets, which the male choristers had taken much pains with, it was perfectly known; but learning that it was now the custom to have the choruses executed before the public *without the chorus singers having once* rehearsed with the orchestra, I experienced a lively inquietude, the more so that but a small number of these gentlemen came to the last rehearsal, and having twice in succession failed to come in after the signal of the orchestra, it was evident that those who were to sing at the concert, without ever having heard the orchestra—that is to say, the majority—would assuredly fail in the same manner. Could I expose them to so unfortunate an accident? Could I expose the Philharmonic Society to a disaster of such gravity? Could I expose myself to see one of the principal *morceaux* of my work compromised in such an attempt? I leave to artists, and to every one who has any knowledge of musical matters, the trouble of answering. As for myself, I do not believe that such experiments should be made in public.

I have the honour to be, Sir,
Your devoted servant,
HECTOR BERLIOZ.

LONDON, 26th *June*, 1855.

The sixth and final concert of the season took place on July 4. Mr. Klindworth, recommended to Dr. Wylde by Wagner, played Henselt's Pianoforte Concerto, and amongst the works performed were Howard Glover's Cantata, "Tam o' Shanter," "Harold in Italy" (Viola Obbligato, Ernst), and the Overture to a MS. Opera, *Abellino*, by M. Praeger.

Three days afterwards Berlioz left London never to return, and not to be heard of again in any prominent way for many years to come. His works disappeared from our programmes; his name was all but forgotten; and if he ever thought of England again, the bitter truth must have come home to him, that, in spite of the "dithyrambs" of the press, and the pyramidal successes he had met with, no permanent impression whatever had been made by his music. Those successes, both with the press and the public, had, indeed, been of a purely personal kind. No one could help admiring and being struck by the characteristic face and figure of the famous composer, expressive of the most ardent zeal for art that ever inspired mortal frame. Much less than this would have been required to call forth that momentary enthusiasm which English audiences, both in London and at provincial festivals, consider it a duty of hospitality to proffer to any composer taking the trouble to conduct his own work, and which would be wholly laudable were it not misleading and, through total want of discrimination, valueless. To apply the well-worn saying about the rocket and the stick to so great a genius as Berlioz would be undignified; let us rather say that he was a meteor rising for a little space above the horizon, illuminating the English heavens, and disappearing again into space. I find that Jullien, faithful to his old gods, introduced the "Invitation à la Valse," as arranged for orchestra by Berlioz, at a "Weber Night" in December, 1857, and on February 13, 1858, the Overture, *Benvenuto Cellini*, and the same

"Invitation à la Valse" were played at the Crystal Palace; the rest is silence for many years.

Time brought its revenges to Berlioz as to other great men; but, as the irony of fate would have it, it was only to his memory. The Franco-German War arose and roused the national feelings of both nations to the highest pitch. That struggle between two of the most musical nations of the world did not produce a single song worth remembering; but when the fight was over music benefited by the popular enthusiasm. It is doubtful whether the Festival plays at Bayreuth would ever have become a reality had Germany not become a unified nation. The French on their side felt the necessity of pitting some musical hero against Beethoven and Wagner, and upon whom could their choice possibly have fallen but upon the much-maligned, much-ridiculed Berlioz? A Berlioz revival accordingly took place in France early in the seventies, and found its echo in England before long. On June 4, 1878, twenty-three years after Berlioz had departed from England, M. Pasdeloup conducted a performance of *Faust* at Her Majesty's Theatre. The audience was scanty, and the overworked chorus of the opera and an Italian tenerino were quite incapable of doing justice to this music, the only bright point in the wretched affair being the singing of Margaret by Madame Minnie Hauck. But wretched though it was, this first performance marked the break of dawn. Sir Charles Hallé brought his Manchester Chorus to London, and revealed the beauties of *Faust* to a Metropolitan public (May 21, 1880). The Crystal Palace, the Richter Concerts, Mr. Barnby, and other conductors followed suit; and to Mr. Cusins belongs the credit of having given the first complete performance of "Romeo and Juliet" (under Berlioz the Finale was always omitted) at a Philharmonic Concert (March 10, 1881). By this time we have heard all Berlioz's important works, excepting the operas, in England, and his name is more or less frequently found in our concert programmes. But has his music, even now, taken firm hold of the masses, as distinguished from the classes, of professional musicians and highly cultured amateurs? I should say not; with the sole exception, perhaps, of *Faust*, which carries the day in all circumstances by dint of its subject. Has the French master's work left any deep or abiding trace on the minds and the workmanship of English musicians? is another question which must, I think, be answered in the negative. I have previously called Berlioz's life a tragedy, and the features of that tragedy may, on a small scale, be observed in the English incident. We see in the hero the same restless craving for notoriety, the eager courting of newspaper praise and the dispensers thereof, the same sanguine exaggeration of success, and the same proneness to obtain that success by the most uncongenial, if not absolutely inartistic means which, in a lesser man, would be almost comic, and which in his case rouse the spectator to the Aristotelian "terror and pity." Berlioz conducting night after night *Lucia*, is a sight not altogether unlike Prometheus tied to his rock. In the best conceivable musical world such a sight of course would not have occurred. Berlioz would have had the means to carry out his gigantic designs placed at his disposal by an admiring community; the State would have mounted his operas and supplied him with as many orchestral players, and as many rehearsals for those players as even he could desire; instead of which he had to rely upon the promises of a charlatan like Jullien, and accept the favours of the keeper of a gambling hell like Bénazet. But the tragedy lay even deeper than this; it affected Berlioz's creative nature. His disposition was, instinctively, somewhat inclined towards the grotesque; he had not that inborn reverence for the proprieties of nature which is the secret of the highest art-achievement. He lacked, in fact, that absolute sincerity which emboldens the artist to do things most outrageous to the commonplace mind, and yet, in themselves, are as consistent as the developments of Nature herself. When Shakespeare's characters talk the most unconventional of dialogues, when Wagner's monsters and dwarfs perform the most gruesome antics, it will be found that they are bound to speak and act thus and not otherwise, according to the manner of their kind. Berlioz set his own individuality above this immutable law. When it suited him to insert a "Hungarian March" in *Faust*, he vaguely argued that amongst the Imperial army there might have been some Hungarians; and when he wanted to give a sequel to his "Fantastic" Symphony, he put together a number of detached pieces written at various times, connecting them with a thread of prose, and thought, or at least wished others to think, that he had created an organic work of art. There was no Act of Parliament, he said to himself, to fetter the artist's freedom. Neither is there. But there is a higher law, the law of nature, by which the free artist is more cogently compelled, than is the pedant by his formulas and his counterpoint. Freedom and license in art are as different as judicious economy and avarice.

It was the same lack of insight into these fundamental actions, which prevented Berlioz from discovering the incompatibility existing between the new subject matter which he introduced into music, and the established forms from which he never freed himself entirely. Hence the want of logical sequence and harmony observable even in his greatest masterpiece, "Romeo and Juliet"; which is neither a Symphony nor a Symphonic Poem, nor an opera, nor a music-drama, although it presents certain features of all these. Liszt, although less endowed with the creative musical gift than Berlioz, felt the necessity of making form and substance agree with each other much more strongly, and in consequence, gave to music what Berlioz never gave it, a most important addition to its structural apparatus—the Symphonic Poem. Berlioz, much more revolutionary in his tendency than Liszt, was much less independent of established formulas, for the reason that he did not allow the law of nature to guide him to freedom. The equation between matter and manner is in his work a question of chance, not of choice. In " Romeo and Juliet," that divinest of elegies, the " Scène d'Amour," is followed later on by a wretched operatic Finale, evidently inspired by the " Bénédiction des Poignards " in the *Huguenots*, and not even a good specimen of its meretricious kind. To Berlioz, in short, music owes an infinite debt of gratitude; he is virtually the creator of the modern orchestra; he has infused a spirit of poetry into music; he has, in fact, written some of the finest music ever written. He has converted platitude by his teaching and example; he has, in fact, made a great many things possible, but he has not established a new starting-point for other artists to rise from and continue the work. Perhaps a play upon words may best explain the difference : Berlioz was a reformer, but not a re—former.

The master's natural bias, let me repeat it once more, was towards the eccentric, the not altogether sincere in art. But that bias might have been toned down and have finally disappeared, had his earlier works met with a little more of the encouragement and intelligent appreciation they so justly deserved. In that case he would have developed himself harmoniously, he would have recognised and acknowledged his own faults, he would have risen on his own dead self as on stepping-stones to higher things. Instead of this, he was almost from the beginning met by a brutal assault and entire want of comprehension on the part of the Parisian public and press, whose faintest praise he would have prized more highly than all the laurels he gathered amongst the Germans and the Russians. This made him reckless, made him desperate. Unable to pacify the critics he defied them, and delighted in doing things which he knew would make them gnash their teeth. The harmonious artist does not think of these things; he listens to a voice, and says what that voice bids him say, regardless of who will listen. Berlioz never attained to that harmony; the tragedy of his life had no Katharsis.

CHAPTER V.

CONCLUSION.

Not many weeks ago I had a conversation with a young English composer in whose future I have, in spite of many disappointments, a singularly firm belief, provided always that he can keep clear of the rocks of commonplace and popularity in the bad sense of the word, to which festival committees, publishers, and other sirens lure the aspiring musician. I was exceedingly struck by the emphatic manner in which my young friend held forth against so-called "absolute" music. The Symphony, the Sonata, and other classical forms appear to him to be the effete types of a bygone age. A piece of music without a subject, he thought, was as meaningless as a picture without a subject. In short, he expressed the most unqualified allegiance to that "poetic idea in music" which Wagner, Liszt, and Berlioz have proclaimed in their various ways.

With this thorough-going revolutionism I was, of course, unable to agree in all its bearings. Ripe experience has taught me that in the house of music there are many habitations, that the classical form created by Haydn, and imbued with infinite varieties and depths of beauty by Mozart, Beethoven, Schumann, Mendelssohn, and many others, is by no means obsolete; that in the hands of genius it may still bring forth rich and noble fruit. Neither can I admit that music must necessarily deal with an extraneous subject; even painting may to a certain extent dispense with such a subject, may become a vague and delightful harmony of colour, as Turner and Mr. Whistler have taught us. Much more so is this the case in the art of sounds. There are some thoughts that lie too deep for words, too deep even for definite realisation; and it is just in expressing these inexpressible things that music shows its most specific power, and ascends from the world of appearances to the world of realities, from the phenomenon to the noumenon, as Plato has it.

It is, on the other hand, equally certain that music, so far from losing any of its power by uniting itself to poetic subject-matter, raises, on the contrary, that subject-matter to its own ideal sphere, and gathers new strength from the union. All modern art of a vital kind runs distinctly in this groove. Beethoven felt the necessity of the poetic idea when he wrote the last movement of the Ninth Symphony, the design of which cannot be explained from any canons of the established classical form. When the master lay on his death-bed, he said: "There is the sketch of a Symphony in my desk—an entirely new idea." That new idea was simply a programme—a programme as definite and as urgently requiring a commensurate innovation of form as any in Liszt's Symphonic Poems. The first movement was to be an "*Andante Cantique* in the old modes, standing either by itself or leading into a fugue." This Adagio was to serve as the key-note, the leit-motive of the entire Symphony. The voices were either to enter early, or else in the last movement after a repetition of the Adagio. Finally, the Greek myth, as embodied in a "Feast to Bacchus," and the Christian faith always represented by the Adagio, were to appear in juxtaposition and in context with each other. The work contained, indeed, all the germs of the most advanced developments of modern music, or of the music of the future, if the reader prefers it. Beethoven here anticipated, at any rate, Liszt and Berlioz, although the step from the symphony to the drama would still have remained to be made had this great work passed out of the embryonic stage.

That the established forms would have gone by the board in this new development there is not the shadow of a doubt; even the fugue which Beethoven intended, although he was doubtful on the matter, would have differed from all other fugues written before or after; it would have been a fugue with a purpose. Established forms, as I said before, would have been broken through; but would the greatest of all masters have, for that reason, created a formless and shapeless thing? No more, surely, than Liszt's Symphonic Poem or Wagner's Dramatic Dialogue are in a higher sense formless and shapeless. If such were the case, their work could not be classified as art, least of all as music, which of its essence is nothing but form.

In this matter of form a distinction should surely be made between the essential and invariable (because inherent to the nature of the art) and the accidental which has grown in the course of time, and therefore must perish and grow again and again; even as leaves and flowers do, although the vital principle which makes them grow remains always the same. Amongst such accidental things, I class, without hesitation, the Symphony. Haydn developed it from the suite, and immortality is his reward; but that surely is no reason why other masters should not unmake it or remake it, as the genius moves them. It is in no sense final; it is not, even in my opinion, perfect of its kind. It lacks balance. Think of these movements in quick time opposed to a single one, in which the most musical, most melancholy element, can find appropriate expression! It is by no means astonishing that in almost every Symphony in existence the weakest movement is the last. Why then should such a form be placed on the pedestal of immutable things like a dogma of the Roman Church? There is, in my opinion, no better reason why a Symphony should have four movements than why a novel should have three volumes.

The matter assumes a very different aspect when we turn from accidental shapes to fundamental principles, unchangeable and indestructible, because organically connected with the nature of the art. Such a principle, for example, is that of repetition, which may be discerned in the simplest tune as well as in the amplest symphonic movement. Another is that of counterpoint and part-writing. Rousseau, in his "Dictionnaire de la Musique," says that it is just as impossible to follow the different parts of a fugue as it is to listen to four people talking at the same time; but in saying so he only shows that although himself the composer of some of the loveliest French songs in existence, he failed to see one of the greatest prerogatives of music—the power of expressing simultaneously various things, of welding divergent elements into one harmonious whole. If Beethoven, or Wagner, or Liszt, or Berlioz had upset the primary laws of their art, I should be the first to call them inspired maniacs—Titans, capable perhaps of knocking down Olympus, but without the power of building it up again. But they of course do nothing of the kind. All that they do is to make these technical resources of music subservient to their poetic purpose; they "borrow," as Pope, the most prosaic of poets, has expressed it, "sound from sense."

It will be seen, then, that my young friend was not altogether wrong when he looked upon a "subject" as the shibboleth and essential characteristic of modern music. That subject, of course, should never lead to physical imitation, pure and simple; neither need it be embodied in definite words. It is not even necessary that the audience should be aware of its existence, as long as the composer feels it and fashions it to his own satisfaction; as long as he determines matter and manner, inspiration and form.

That a highly gifted young Englishman should be more or less articulately conscious of these things, is surely a significant fact. It led me considerably to modify the opinion, frequently expressed in these pages of the slight effect which the strivings of Wagner, of Liszt, and of Berlioz have had upon English music, and I close my book with the query: Is it possible that our young idea is shooting in the spirit of these masters, that in England also an era of the music of the future is at hand?

THE END.

For EU product safety concerns, contact us at Calle de José Abascal, 56–1°,
28003 Madrid, Spain or eugpsr@cambridge.org.

www.ingramcontent.com/pod-product-compliance
Ingram Content Group UK Ltd.
Pitfield, Milton Keynes, MK11 3LW, UK
UKHW041952230426
12048UKWH00008B/297